IDYLL OF THE KINGS

1889–1979

The story of the King Line its ships and the men who sailed and managed them

by

ALAN S. MALLETT

Published by the World Ship Society
Kendal LA9 7LT
1980

ISBN 0 905617 10 X

FOREWORD

by Sir Nicholas Cayzer, Bt.—Chairman, King Line Limited

Between the middle and the end of the nineteenth century and with the transition from sail to steam many household names in the shipping world appeared—Cunard, P & O, Ocean Steam, Union-Castle and so on—and in each case they were connected with an individual of initiative and drive, in most cases coming from very humble beginnings. Not so in the case of the first Lord Kylsant, the founder of the King Line. He was the third son of a Canon of Salisbury Cathedral, Sir James Philipps, twelfth Baronet.

You will read in Mr. Mallett's "Idyll of the Kings" the story of the King Line and the changes that took place over the years 1889 to 1979. I came to know the King Line when the Clan Line merged with Union-Castle in 1956, and from being a tramp Company King Line is now represented by five bulk carriers.

I hope that Mr. Mallett's book will be read by all those who were connected with the King Line over the years and by a wider public that has always followed the fortunes of British shipping with interest.

Owen Cosby Philipps, 1904

The Hon. Mrs. N. D. Fisher-Hoch

Beginnings—Philipps, Philipps and Co. Ltd.

Owen Cosby Philipps, third son of the Rev. Canon Sir James Erasmus Philipps, twelfth baronet and Canon of Salisbury Cathedral, was born at Warminster on March 25th, 1863. The Philipps family is one of the oldest in the country—shortly after the Norman Conquest the then head of the family, Cadifor ap Colwyn, Lord of Dyvett, took upon himself the style of Lord of Kylsant, but in fact the family are able to trace their ancestry back through ancient Princes of Dyfed as far as A.D. 50. The young Owen attended school at Newton Abbot, and, soon after his seventeenth birthday, commenced his business career in the Newcastle offices of Dent and Co., Shipbrokers. In 1886 he moved to Glasgow and three years later was able to promote a new company, registered on July 23rd, 1889, to own and operate a small steamship managed by himself trading as Philipps and Co., later Philipps, Philipps and Co. Ltd.

The new company was named King Alfred Steamship Co. Ltd. the name being chosen for his next younger brother, Alfred Perrott Philipps, born in 1864. Records now available do not indicate whether or not it was Owen Philipps' intention that his brother should join him in his new venture, although the fact that the company bore his name and that for the next twenty years only two King Line vessels bore non-Welsh names lends credence to the possibility that this was so. However, it was not to be. On the date of the company's incorporation Alfred Philipps was on the point of leaving Canada where he had been visiting with another brother. On August 8th, 1889 he fell overboard and drowned, and if the original intention had been for him to have been involved with the company, his place was taken by his eldest brother, John Wynford Philipps, subsequently Viscount St. Davids.

A steamship under construction at Blyth was purchased for £15,680, named "King Alfred" and entered service in September 1889 under the command of Captain J. J. Hebron, himself a shareholder in the new company. The new ship earned sufficient to warrant payment of a 3% dividend in February 1890, and a further 3% in September 1890. She was to trade successfully until her loss by stranding in 1894.

A second vessel was acquired in 1893, necessitating a change of name by the company to King Line Ltd. and by 1900 a further six vessels had been added to the fleet, financed by regular increases of capital. Furthermore, a second company, Scottish Steamship Co. Ltd. was incorporated in 1896. A single ship company for most of its career, its ships bore the names of Scottish Kings. Additionally it was about this time that Owen Philipps formed London Maritime Investment Co. Ltd. and became involved with the old-established London and Thameshaven Oil Wharves Ltd. a company concerned with oil storage along the Thames and at Le Havre.

The colour scheme adopted for the fleet was black hull and yellow ochre funnel with black tops. Originally the superstructure and masts were light fawn, but subsequently the superstructure was painted white until 1945, when a return was made to the original scheme, although after 1959 all vessels adopted Clan line colouring until 1977. Naturally on occasions funnels were repainted in charterer's colours. The house flag adopted was a lion rampant bearing a gold collar and chain, and in the nineteen-twenties it was the popular belief, at any rate amongst sea-going staff, that this emblem was adopted in honour of the company's Scottish registration, the gold collar and chain being considered symbolic of Welsh domination, and the whole being irreverently referred to as a "puppy dancing on a sausage". The factual origin of the flag is far more interesting, as it is the emblem of the Philipps Coat of Arms, originally a Black Lion Rampant. The addition of a gold collar and chain was granted by Richard Coeur de Lion when knighting Aron ap Rhys, an ancestor of Owen Philipps' for bravery in the Crusades, and the motto, also adopted by Owen Philipps after his elevation to the peerage, was "Ducit amor patriae". By one of those uncanny coincidences, the founders of Clan Line had eleven years earlier adopted a Red Lion Rampant as their emblem, a coincidence that was to bear some significance in later years.

John Philipps' interests included The Buenos Aires and Pacific Railway Co. Ltd., for which the shipment of coal was to provide lucrative employment not only for the "Kings" but also for the railway company's own fleet of "Dons" and that of the Court Line, established by another brother.

KING FREDERICK (1) on trials   *Tyne & Wear County Council*

The last year of the old century saw the completion of Owen Philipps' first "take-over" bid, by the acquisition of the share capital of Northern Transport Ltd. for £60,000 late in 1900 from Petersen, Tate, who, however, continued to manage the fleet of three small vessels until 1902, when these ships were transferred to King Line ownership and Philipps, Philipps & Co. management, while Northern Transport Ltd. was put into voluntary liquidation. The largest of the steamers, a tanker, subsequently foundered in September 1903 with heavy loss of life during a hurricane of exceptional severity.

The two smaller vessels acquired merit some attention. Few who served aboard the "Kings" in the opening years of the twentieth century realised that their company owned two small passenger carrying vessels, but this is what "Barnstable" and "Brookline" were. Built at Middlesbrough under supervision of Captain Anderson for long charter to the Boston Fruit Company, they were completed in 1894. The transfer of ownership a few years later did not affect them, since their entire career was spent on the Jamaica–Baltimore or Boston run, where their 75,000 cu. ft. cargo capacity equivalent to 35,000 stems of bananas, 13 knots speed and elegant accommodation for 24 passengers enabled them, as was intended, to surpass anything previously built for the service. Ventilation was provided for the fruit by natural means. They remained profitable to owners and charterers alike throughout their seventeen years service, after which both returned to England, to lay up in Sharpness until, 1913, they were sold for breaking up, leaving behind memories of their proud place in the history of "The Great White Fleet" as their charterers were ultimately to become.

A year later Owen Philipps offered to buy Tyne Steam Shipping Co. Ltd., then established for 37 years. Profits had varied between £12,000 and £16,000 in the 5 years to 1899, paying a $6\frac{1}{2}$% dividend for each year, and in 1900 these increased to £27,000 and the dividend to $7\frac{1}{2}$%. Philipps' offer totalled £360,000 tied to a condition that on purchase he should become chairman of Tyne Steam Shipping Co. Ltd. Negotiations dragged on for eleven months before they were abandoned.

Glimpses of detail appear in the Minute Books and elsewhere from time to time. In the early years of the century "King Frederick" and "King David" were time chartered at £1,025 per month for two years and £1,100 per month for one year respectively. The

Scottish Steamship Co. sold the "King Edgar" at a profit of £4,998 in 1901 and a distribution of 25% was made to shareholders. The company, paid-up capital £15,200, had cash and investments totalling £27,590 and was seeking another ship. King Line had experimented with oil fuel in one of their steamers and the result was most satisfactory both as regards speed and economy of operation (Chairman's statement 1904). Unfortunately further trials in Northern waters proved less satisfactory as the tanks were not fitted with adequate heating and the experiment was abandoned.

KING DAVID (2)   *World Ship Photo Library*

In May 1905 it was decided to replace the fleet. Thirty builders tendered for the ten 6-7000 ton dwt steamers specified, costing about £47,500 each, for the King Line and Scottish Steamship Co. as well as several others for the Court Line and Buenos Aires and Pacific Railway Co. Four of the ships carried 7,200 tons dwt, and the remainder 6,200 tons. Probably hundreds of tramps were built to the same basic "built by the mile, cut off by the fathom and the ends hammered in" design. They had four holds with large main deck hatches clear of obstructions suitable for bulk grain or coal, served by 10 derricks, with another two to serve the main bunker hatch abaft the bridge. Living conditions were, by current standards, almost neolithic, with no electric generator or lighting—only oil, and no heating arrangements other than a stove in the saloon. Captain A. R. Williamson, who went on to follow a highly successful career with Jardine, Matheson, joined "King Howel" as one of four apprentices for her maiden voyage towards the end of 1906, to commence his three years indentures, at £5 for the first year, rising annually to £8 and £12 plus a £10 bonus for satisfactory completion of service. Captain Williamson was then just over 15 years of age. The "King Howel" was manned by 28 men—3 Deck Officers including the Master, 3 Engineer Officers, 4 Apprentices, Bosun, Carpenter, 5 ABs, 6 Firemen, 2 Trimmers, a Steward a Cook and a Donkeyman. Navigational equipment consisted of a standard compass—fitted on a pole mounted on a small circular platform to minimise magnetic interference, one steering compass, one chronometer, patent log and patent sounding machine. There was also, on the poop, a rudder extension plate known as the "Danube" rudder, essential for manoeuvrability in that fast running river with close turns and no tugs.

Captain Williamson recalled that during his indentures the habitual routine was that from Spring to Autumn "King Howel" would ship coal from Welsh ports to the Mediterranean, usually Port Said, and proceeding thence in ballast to the Black Sea to load grain for U.K. or North European ports. By late autumn, with the Ukrainian harvests gathered, it was coal for the River Plate and grain homewards. As the ship's speed, fully laden, was about 8 knots, a River Plate trip lasted three months. Very occasionally a

Officers of KING HOWEL, 1907 *Captain A. R. Williamson*

Spring voyage might be varied by a charter to proceed, after discharging at Port Said, to Bombay or Karachi. In heavy weather it was customary to set staysails in order to minimise rolling, a matter of some concern when carrying grain in bulk and enjoying limited freeboard. Capt. Williamson's master was Captain W. Davies, who eventually retired in 1929 and who had commenced his sea-going career as a carpenter. Towards the end of 1908 Captain Davies and "Chips" decided that an upper bridge would undoubtedly improve "King Howel" as the open bridge with its brass wheel was a nightmare in cold weather. The necessary materials were assembled but Captain Williamson's indentures expired before execution of the plan, which was evidently successful as Captain Davies subsequently modified "King Edward" in like manner.

Only two of these ten ships remained in service after 1918, one of which— "King John"—survived as the "Antonio Castro" until 1970 when her owners wrote:

ANTONIO CASTRO at Laguna, South Brazil *Courtesy of the owners*

"This excellent ship, whose history you so well know, was acquired by our firm in 1962 from the firm "Luciano de Castro & Cia. Ltd." (owners of the ship from 1952 till 1962, and who named the ship "Antonio Castro") being her first voyage at our service in June of the same year. Since then, the mentioned ship, always well cared for by us, performed her voyages normally and satisfactorily, operating only in coasting from North to South of Brazil, loading salt, coffee and wood, till February 1970, when owing to a fire aboard, in port at Cabedelo—North of Brazil, the ship was practically destroyed without any possibility of recuperation. Thus, I am sorry to say, this old, and till then, efficient ship, with 64 years of good service, had to be sold in September 1970, for demolition purposes.
Enclosed are two photographs of the S/S "ANTONIO CASTRO" in her "full swing" at service of our Company—having obtained in Brazilian Cabotage an index of productivity truly surprising, in accordance with the statistics of Brazilian Merchant Marine.
Believe us, dear sir, S/S "ANTONIO CASTRO" will be always remembered by our firm with affection".

The financing of this new fleet absorbed much time, but eventually in 1908 it was decided to sub-divide the £10 shares in £1 shares and to raise a further £100,000 by way of $5\frac{1}{2}\%$ Cumulative Preference Shares. The latter proposal was subsequently replaced by £200,000 $5\frac{1}{2}\%$ Debenture Bonds secured by a First Mortgage on the fleet, redeemed shortly before hostilities commenced in 1914.

The relationship between Owen Philipps' King Line and Scottish Steamship Co. and the two companies directed by his brothers was very close despite lack of any formal connections by way of shareholding. The railway fleet was managed by George Dodd, a friend of Owen Philipps since they first met at Dents, and Lloyds Register reveals that several captains commanded both "Kings" and "Dons" between 1906 and 1914. Furthermore, Court Line ships did not carry apprentices until the 1930's and consequently drew their officers from King Line.

Early in 1912 a new steamer of 7-8000 tons dwt suitable for general cargo service or with "any of the companies connected with the Chairman" was considered but not proceeded with on account of "high building costs". In 1903 Owen Philipps had been appointed Chairman of the Royal Mail Steam Packet Company. Inheriting an incredibly out-dated fleet, he succeeded not only in substantially modernising it by 1913, but also in acquiring the Shire Line, the Elder Dempster Line and the Pacific Steam Navigation Company, and early in 1912 was negotiating the purchase of the Union-Castle Line. His services to British Shipping were recognised when he was created K.C.M.G. in 1908. These services included pioneer work concerning defensive armament of merchant vessels, ultimately resulting in his being appointed an Honorary Captain in the Royal Naval Volunteer Reserve, and also his participation in the Royal Commission on Shipping Rings.

In August 1914 King Line and Scottish Steamship Company owned 9 vessels. Two were sold during the War and 5 sunk, the first being "King Lud" which on September 25th, 1914 had the doubtful distinction of being captured by S.M.S. "Emden" aboard which a relation of the Kaiser, H.I.H. Franz Joseph, Prince of Hohenzollern, was serving as Second Torpedo Officer. After transferring edible stores, "King Lud's" crew were transferred to the prize vessel "Markomannia" and "King Lud" was scuttled. Another vessel, "King David", was torpedoed in 1917 while transporting ammunition but all the crew survived, despite 5 days and 6 nights in open boats.

During the war King Line traded profitably with dividends increasing from 8% to 16% in 1917, although a year later this dropped to 12%. A shareholder's suggestion that all or part of the fleet be sold and that the company be wound up or part of the capital be repaid, was rejected in January 1916. The idea was not, however, entirely without point. "King Frederick" had been sold for £36,250 in January 1915. A year later, her sister ship "King Howel" realised £97,500. She had been time-chartered to the Bay S.S. Co. which itself had re-chartered her to the French Government and the sale arose as a result of a clause in the charter party providing for sale in the event of the vessel being delayed in excess of a certain period. At the time of sale she was frozen-up in Hudsons Bay.

Sir Owen Philipps' views became clear in April 1917 when the authorised share capital was doubled to £1,000,000. Two years later Treasury approval was sought for the issue of 150,000 shares at a premium of £1 to be applied to the purchase of War-Standard ships the first of which was delivered on 21st November, 1919 and, appropriately enough for the start of a new era, the name "King Alfred" was revived. The "King John" was then sold for £150,000, close on four times her building cost. In March 1920, the company contracted with Harland & Wolff to build two fabricated "N" type vessels but this contract was cancelled at a cost of £12,000. One "N" type ship, the "Glenspey", one of several allocated to the R.M.S.P. and its associated companies, was acquired. Renamed "King Bleddyn" and converted to burn oil fuel, she was the company's largest vessel to date. She was not particularly successful, being deemed both under-powered and extravagant on fuel. The murder of an Engineer Officer on board did not enhance her reputation and not surprisingly she was afterwards believed to be haunted.

As if this was not enough, "King Bleddyn" proved accident-prone throughout her career. In the early 1920's she grounded on the Whale Rock off Robben Island, but unusually, she was pulled off and, making water forward much faster than any bilge pump could contain, towed across Table Bay to the docks. The South African Railways and Harbour Board were normally chary of admitting ships in such condition lest they sink in the dock entrance, but in this case no objections were raised, and soon "King Bleddyn" was on the muddy dock floor alongside No. 7 Quay, discharging her cargo, which strange to say happened to be railway lines from Halifax, Nova Scotia, consigned for the South African Railways. After laying-up for most of the early 1930's she was sold in 1937, and, to the surprise of many, survived the Second World War, to end her days in two pieces in 1954 when, laden with iron ore, she grounded off Bats in the Schelde estuary.

KING DAVID   *Alex Duncan*

A third acquisition, renamed "King David", was built in 1912, for the Hamburg Bremer-Afrika Line as "Gundomar". Of a size similar to the pre-war vessels, her amenities included accommodation for 12 passengers, adapted by King Line for the officers, and 40 derricks and a nest of surf-boats for the West African trade. She was however, too small to be really satisfactory for post-war conditions, and additionally was heavy on fuel. In 1931 she was laid up, and made few voyages until her sale in 1938. Subsequently, as the "Miramar" she was one of a dozen vessels whose registration was suspended by the Panamanian Government in 1952 for trading with Communist China, in which country's waters she ended her days some ten years later.

During the immediate period following the Armistice, Philipps, Philipps & Co. Ltd. managed four ex-enemy steamers on behalf of His Majesty's government, enabling at least some of the sea-going staff to remain in employment pending full post-war reconstruction of the fleet.

Lord Kylsant—The Years of Expansion

By the time that King Line passed its thirtieth anniversary, Sir Owen's activities, especially the R.M.S.P. and allied concerns, had increased substantially and had broadened into charitable and political fields including trusteeship of the Royal Alfred Aged Merchant Seamen's Institution, and membership of the Executive Committee of King George's Fund for Sailors and King Edward's Hospital Fund. He was Chairman of the Wales and Monmouthshire Conservative and Unionist Council, and had served as a Member of Parliament for many years. His financial advice to the Church in Wales had revitalised their finances and substantially improved the living standards of the Welsh clergy. A man of fine presence, standing 6'6" and always immaculately dressed, he was endowed with exceptional energy and capabilities, enhanced by a natural charm of manner which gained him substantial loyalty from his employees. He worked from early morning to late at night on his various interests, his ambition being to build, under the Red Ensign, the world's finest and greatest shipping organisation, for he was intensely patriotic. At the end of the Great War he resumed his efforts to strengthen these interests and assisted the Government, in association with Lord Inchcape, by eventually acquiring seventy-seven standard vessels at a cost of over fifteen million pounds. His services were publicly recognised in 1918 with his elevation to G.C.M.G., followed in 1923 when he was created Baron Kylsant of Carmarthen, and a year later with his appointment as Lord Lieutenant of Haverfordwest.

Meanwhile, day-to-day management of King Line fell on other shoulders, formally recognised in 1923 when Dodd, Thomson & Co. Ltd. succeeded Philipps, Philipps & Co. Ltd. as Managers of King Line and Scottish Steamship Co. Lord Kylsant remained Chairman and retained responsibility for financial control and acquisition of new tonnage, although his interest was, and remained, much deeper. Mr. Lindsay Dryden, when Second Engineer aboard one of the steamers in the twenties, recalls that when he was working in the shaft tunnel he heard someone approaching. It was Lord Kylsant, stooping in the cramped space. From time to time surplus funds were invested in other companies of which he was Chairman, principally the R.M.S.P. His private secretary during the twenties, John Bevan, recalls that he regularly telephoned the King Line office early each morning to talk first to Sir Vernon, who was responsible for chartering, and then to George Dodd, responsible for administration.

George Dodd was a lifelong friend and colleague of Lord Kylsant. They first met in the 1880's when both were employed by Dent's in Newcastle. Little is known of George Dodd thereafter, except that he was an enthusiastic rugby player, until he went into partnership in Newcastle in 1901 trading as Dodd, Morrison & Co., managers of a small coaster S.S. "Waverley", a photograph of which vessel hung in George Dodd's office until his death. In January 1904 he was admitted to the Baltic Exchange where he was considered to be one of the best dressed men, and, when the Buenos Aires and Pacific Railway built its own fleet of "Don" vessels in 1905–1906, it was Lord Kylsant's old friend who, trading as George Dodd & Co., was appointed fleet manager.

His appointment to the King Line board in November 1918 followed the sale of the sole railway ship to survive the War. A blunt, hard-headed extrovert North Englander, George Dodd was essentially a practical man, who entered his office at 9.00 a.m. precisely and would interview Junior Officers immediately, Captains being seen at 9.30 a.m. He had no time for verbosity, letters exceeding more than one small sheet of paper were invariably tossed into the waste-paper basket with an explosive "I haven't time to read all that", to the distress of the Secretary Mr. Matthews, who had afterwards to salvage them. His own correspondence was the soul of brevity. Captain George Smith, O.B.E., still has the only letter he ever received from George Dodd exceeding one page.

A diversion to Antwerp had coincided with Captain Smith's wedding plans—and the necessary change in arrangements had beaten even George Dodd. Captain Smith remembers George Dodd as "down to earth, very practical and cost conscious—not mean but economical. I think his earlier experiences left him with a horror of bankruptcy. No unnecessary expense would be sanctioned. In the late twenties, he used often to enquire how the company could further economise—my reply was invariably "fit refrigerators" until one was fitted aboard "King Edward", placed in the after starboard corner of the bridge space above the 'tween deck bunkers with direct entry off the well deck, with the machinery in an adjoining compartment, all of which were subject to immersion by sea water in inclement weather. Certainly the siting left much to be desired, as the thing was constantly breaking down, and George Dodd at one point said in jest "if you mention refrigerators again Captain Smith I'll throw you out the window", but we got them, in 1932".

In fairness it ought to be added that Captain A. J. MacInnes served a year of his apprenticeship aboard "King Edward" in 1927, and despite a couple of instances of flooding, leading to the loss of beef, pork etc. he recalls that the ship's company were very proud of their refrigerator.

Assisting George Dodd was the Secretary, Mr. Matthews, a self-effacing but very efficient Company Secretary, Miss Alice Axten, then responsible for accounts and personnel records, Mr. L. H. Hatt, a brilliant mathematician, and Mr. A. H. Scarf, joined in 1924 by Mr. A. G. Preston, both junior clerks.

The other new Director, Sir Vernon Thomson, K.B.E., was a Scotsman. One of four brothers, his father died while he was very young and his mother had worked hard to raise the young family. In 1897 he became office boy at Philipps, Philipps and Co. Ltd. Within five years he was daily negotiating charters on the Baltic and when thirty years old, was appointed a director of Philipps, Philipps, & Co. Ltd. in 1911. Ten years later he became a director of King Line. During the war he served the Ministry of Shipping as Assistant Director of the Ship Management branch, for which services he was created K.B.E. in 1919. In 1923 he became Chairman of the Documentary Committee of the Chamber of Shipping, a post he held for twelve years. Under his chairmanship several charter parties were re-negotiated as well as some new forms, including the "Austral" charter relating to the carriage of grain between Australia and the UK, a trade in which King Line was just entering, and which was to prove of the utmost significance in years to come. His principal assistant was Oscar Hall, who had joined Philipps, Philipps & Co. Ltd. in 1911.

Captain Smith recalls Sir Vernon in those years with vivid clarity—"He had the sharpest intellect of any man I know—only John Buchan could match him, but with one important difference—John Buchan spoke more slowly, leaving one time to think, whereas Sir Vernon in pursuit of information resembled an ultra-efficient machine-gun, firing questions in all directions at a fantastic rate. I remember preparing detailed notes on a draft charter party then under consideration which Sir Vernon read overnight and discussed the following day with his legal advisers. He then sent for me. I suppose the paperwork stood some inches high, but without even looking at it, he started "Now you start by saying . . ." and, that point being exhausted, "your next point is . . ." and so it went on. Now these were highly complicated legal points, but he had it all in his head. He went through the lot word perfect, without so much as a glance. His clear headedness and total grasp of the business was incredible". A view expressed by all who worked with Sir Vernon.

Captain Smith himself had an eventful career. Joining King Line in 1917 to complete his indentures, after a spell at Greenwich and a brief apprenticeship interrupted by torpedo, he became 3rd officer at 18, 2nd officer at 20, Chief Officer at 23 and Master at 27. "Much was expected of us—promotion was on merit rather than on seniority—but, one slip and you were out. There were no second chances in those days. Captains were expected to be omniscient—in business and legal matters as well as in seamanship and navigation. You would sail with orders to proceed southwards for further instructions—which never came—so at a certain point you would cable "Am proceeding to Australia" and heaven help you if it should have been Argentina. It was your decision. Of course, you would build up your contacts in the ports you visited, and this would often influence your decision. The most you could expect from the Company was "Thank you". They didn't pay my fares up when I was working on those Charter parties, or even offer me lunch—and leave was unpaid in those days. It was simply expected of you. "Just but not generous" was how King Line was described. You might wonder why we carried on working for them when we could have earned far more elsewhere. Well, the answer is that they were gentlemen. You knew exactly where you stood with them. They had integrity and were efficient managers. Not that they were mean—but waste was never tolerated. The ships were always perfectly maintained, because it was more economical. Sir Vernon was a man of austere personal tastes—no smoking, no drinking, he was devoted to his mother, whom he supported for the remainder of her life. He was privately a generous and deeply religious man, though few realised it. He spent his annual holiday in Scotland and during the depression he would return with one or two unemployed lads who would sign on for King Line, and some became excellent seamen. George Dodd was far more out-going although the memory of his early years never left him, and I think he had other problems. Both were very strong, forceful characters, but they would always listen to what their Captains had to say, and that was worth a great deal."

The fleet was enlarged in 1923. Five standard-type vessels built in Hong Kong were acquired after the bankruptcy of the former owners, and a further two a year or so later. The shortage of shipping had become a glut when "King Edward", last of the pre-war ships, was sold in 1924 realising only £27,000.

With further expansion in mind, two efforts were to prove unsuccessful. An offer to acquire the Adam fleet, 4 war-built steamers of 7,500 tons dwt. for £160,000 failed, as did, shortly afterwards, an offer of £275,000 for 8 similar vessels owned by Gould Steamships and Industrials Ltd., declined by the receivers scarcely an hour before it was to go to the Court for approval, following receipt of a rival bid for £300,000.

A third attempt proved successful. The Canadian Government, seeking to counter the liner conference system operating the Canadian routes, revived a scheme originally put forward in association with Sir William Petersen in 1897, but dropped in the following year, and announced that provisional terms had been agreed with Sir William Petersen whereby the latter would provide a regular service between the UK and European ports and Canada. Rates were fixed by the Canadian Government at substantially lower levels than those of the Conference lines. 10 ships were to be built at a cost of £1.2 million, and the agreement provided, *inter alia*, for the installation of passenger accommodation and for chilled freight compartments, and Sir William Petersen was to receive an annual subsidy of £275,000. This agreement, announced in 1925, naturally aroused strong opposition from the Conference lines, as well as doubts on the practical possibilities of building the stipulated fleet on the lines indicated at the stated cost. Schedule A to the agreement mentioned that two vessels (without passenger accommodation or chilled compartments) were then building at D. & W. Henderson's Glasgow yard (a subsidiary of Harland & Wolff Ltd.).

Unfortunately for Sir William matters did not go smoothly. In May 1925 he travelled to Ottawa to discuss the arrangements, by now a major political issue. On June 12th Sir William died, and the Canadian Government announced the abandonment of its plans, leaving Hendersons with two ships on their hands. Sir William's net estate, announced on 30th July, amounted to nil. On 6th August the British Motorship Co. Ltd. was registered, nominal capital £100,000 and in November King Line applied for, and received, 10,000 shares at par. It is not clear whether this company was originally intended to own the substantial number of diesel engined tramps Lord Kylsant was planning to build, but in the event only the two vessels building at Henderson's sailed under its house-flag. British Motorship Co. traded until 1935, when its fleet was transferred to Scottish Steamship Co.

The two ships then building were to have been named "River Ottawa" and "River St. Lawrence", but were in fact named "King James" and "King Malcolm", the first named being well-remembered in particular by Captain A. J. MacInnes who not only served the first eighteen months of his apprenticeship aboard her, joining her at the yard on 19th November, 1925, but who in 1938 became her Chief Officer, and in 1943 Master. When Capt. MacInnes began his service his annual remuneration was £10, increasing year by year to £12, £18 and £20, which sums, to which was added a bonus of £5 for satisfactory completion of indentures, totalled £65 for four years.

The construction of the ships was known as the "Monitor" type, a conglomeration of conventional Isherwood and other designs. Externally the outstanding features were the flush deck, three masts, the placing of two hatches between bridge and funnel, not often encountered, and the "corrugations"—two blisters either side running the length of the hull-devised on the theory that the concave shape between them would channel water towards the propeller, thereby improving speed at no extra cost in fuel. Constructionally, the straight sided sections in the shelter deck space had conventional framing some two feet apart whilst the corrugated section had framing five feet apart, the deck beams running both longitudinally and transversely.

Captain R. H. Evans

Captain G. F. Smith

The theory behind the corrugations did not work out in practice as speed fully laden rarely exceeded 10 knots on 8 tons of diesel daily, as against 11 knots anticipated, whilst under war-time conditions "King James" was pressed to maintain station in convoys steaming over 8 knots. Consequently she usually joined $7\frac{1}{2}$ knot convoys in which she was sometimes chosen as Commodore Ship. Moreover, the corrugations were susceptible to damage from hitting wharves while docking, or from pilot tenders trying to tranship pilots. Thirdly, the fact that the upper part of the vessel tended to give more in a seaway than the more rigid corrugated sections must have imposed stresses which contributed to the not infrequent times when the hulls cracked at sea—which eventually was to lead to "King James's" loss in 1960. An additional problem, rectified at an early stage, was a propensity to roll. Bilge keels solved that one.

Nonetheless, Captain MacInnes recalls "I spent eight years in the old "King James" and with all her faults I had a great affection for the ship. There weren't many tramps in 1925 which were diesel-propelled with all electric gear and no steam at all, and we were quite a news item in the American press when we loaded a full cargo of bulk wheat at Tacoma for Belfast and Limerick. We were all very proud of her". The ships were bought for the low price of £25,000 each—whether the fact that Lord Kylsant was also Chairman of Harland and Wolff had anything to do with it or whether nobody else wanted these unusual ships, is not known.

Lord Kylsant was an early advocate of diesel propulsion. Already he had ordered three liners of 20,000 tons each for his South American and South African services. Now he pressed ahead with his plans for a diesel-engined tramp fleet, albeit of a more conventional design. Nine vessels, three flush deckers, four three-island vessels, and two three-island vessels with 'tween decks, were built, emerging from Belfast in that order at monthly intervals from November 1927 to July 1928, and, after initial troubles with the engine bed-plating, speedily rectified at the builders' expense, settled down to long and trouble-free service. John Bevan was afterwards to describe this programme as "one of the master strokes in the history of the King Line" and there can be no doubt that these ships' ability to carry 7,500 tons of cargo at 10 knots on $7\frac{1}{2}$ tons fuel daily and $6\frac{1}{4}$ tons in ballast substantially carried the company through the thirties.

The new motorships cost £969,500 and the financing was the outcome of prolonged negotiation in 1926, as a result of which the Advisory Committee set up by the Trade Facilities Acts secured a loan of £800,000 from the Northern Ireland Government, at 5 per cent interest. The loan was to be repaid in 8 annual instalments of £89,000 and one of £88,000, commencing on January 31st, 1931, and secured by mortgage on the nine new ships and on three of the steamers, although in the event the repayment provisions were revised in 1934 and honoured ahead of schedule.

KING ARTHUR   *World Ship Photo Library*

The year after the last ship "King William", was commissioned, the company sustained its most recent peacetime loss, The Melbourne Gas Company, subsidised by the Australian Government, had contracted for several ship-loads of Gas coal from Fife, one of which cargoes was loaded by "King Cadwallon" at Methil, in May 1929. On 9th July fire broke out off the South African coast and the crew had to abandon the ship, which eventually drifted ashore near East London. Five months later, a second vessel, the "Siltonhall" which ironically had taken the crew off the blazing "King Cadwallon" was herself lost in similar circumstances. On the same charter Captain Smith commanding "King Alfred" after sustaining heavy weather damage in freak gales, put into Albany with fires in Numbers 2 and 4 holds, which fortunately were extinguished by the crew, saving the company the expense of ten days attendance by the Albany Fire Brigade during unloading, and "King Howel" suffered similarly after an eighty-eight day passage from Scotland to Port Pirie although again little damage resulted.

At the 1929 Annual General Meeting Lord Kylsant had told shareholders "It is 40 years since I founded the King Line. The Company has had its fluctuations of alternate prosperity and depression but it can be fairly claimed that a sound conservative financial policy had been pursued, as a result of which while no sensational dividends have been paid shareholders have received a moderate but regular return upon their capital.... There are signs that the volume of trade is again slowly on the upgrade...."

Unfortunately, the signs referred to by Lord Kylsant were premature, and his own group, which controlled two million tons of shipping, suffered in consequence. King Line paid a dividend of 7 per cent for the year 1929, maintaining the average to that year, but it was the last for some time. In October 1931, Lord Kylsant resigned all his offices, including the Chairmanship of the King Line.

**KING ROBERT, KING STEPHEN and KING WILLIAM (left to right),
loading wheat at Williamstown, Victoria *ca.* 1934**   *Captain A. J. MacInnes*

The circumstances of Lord Kylsant's resignation are well-known and of only incidental relevance to this narrative. Briefly, he was convicted under the Larceny Act 1861 of publishing a prospectus which "he knew to be false in a material particular", in that although every figure and every word in the prospectus was true, the prospectus conveyed a false impression insofar as it implied that the issuing Company (the R.M.S.P.) was trading at a profit when, in fact, it had not done so for some years and that the favourable balances shown had been arrived at only after writing back reserves no longer required. Conviction under Section 84 of the Act hinged upon the Judge's direction to the Jury to the effect that a written statement might be false within the meaning of the Section not only because of what it stated but also because of what it concealed or omitted or implied.

Lord Kylsant bore his trial with dignity, gentleness and consideration for others, taking the whole responsibility on to his own shoulders. His demeanour earned him considerable public sympathy at the time, and many who knew him intimately would have sworn that he never had any intention of defrauding anybody, and that it had never occurred to him that by including in the prospectus information as published in the company's accounts he was acting dishonestly. In this connection it is a fact that he was acquitted of a charge relating to the publication of false accounts, on the grounds that the preparation and publication of public company accounts on that basis was fully within the provision of the law at that time. On his return to Wales he was welcomed home by all the local people and, John Bevan recollects, often appeared in public supremely conscious of his innocence. Lord Kylsant died in June 1937, but with the knowledge that the ships he had built and the men he had recruited for his first company had together borne it through the traumatic years following his departure.

Dodd, Thomson & Co. Ltd.—Through the Storm

Sir Vernon Thomson succeeded Lord Kylsant—it may be wondered why George Dodd, the senior director, did not become chairman, but this is probably explained by their respective ages, 50 years as against 70. The new Chairman's lot was an unenviable one, save that now Lord Kylsant's motorships came into their own. For four years, from 1931, to 1934, these nine ships remained in service while their steam-powered sisters were generally laid up. It is fruitless but nonetheless fascinating to speculate on what the situation might have been had the Gould offer succeeded, landing King Line with eight further steamers. Would the motorships have been built, or would substantially greater sums have been invested in R.M.S.P.? Certainly the disguise had now fallen from that particular blessing. After the managers reduced their fees by 50%, the motorships earned an average of £4,000–£4,500 voyage profits annually apiece. One third of this was devoted to maintaining the laid-up steamers, and the remainder to loan interest and depreciation. Nothing was left for the shareholders as the conservative financial policy followed by Lord Kylsant was maintained. One substantial and sad entry appeared in the 1931 accounts. For many years King Line had invested varying sums in R.M.S.P. stocks. The need to fund £170,000 towards the new motorships had greatly reduced these investments, but the remaining £170,200 had to be written off against the General Reserve.

Capt. J. A. Lewis recalls the thirties. After early service aboard "King Stephen" he went ashore in April 1932 to sit his Masters Certificate. In September 1933 he was offered employment afloat, as Night-Watchman aboard "King Bleddyn", laid up at Belfast, at 40 pence a night "but it was a job". It lasted 5 months. Later, from August 1935 to January 1936, he was promoted to Officer-in-Charge of "King David" at Sunderland—at £10 per month plus 20 pence per day subsistence. Only then did the opportunity to use his certificate arrive, when he was appointed Chief Officer of the ship he had left four years earlier. His experience must be one of many seeking employment in those days. To get the quoted salaries into proportion it should be noted that King Line then paid their captains £25 per month (or £30 per month on the motorships), Chief Engineers receiving £23.50 or £29 respectively. Once at sea again, "mostly we were engaged on the Austral Charters. Bunkering at Las Palmas en route to Australia we could then complete the round voyage to the U.K. with a full cargo, albeit at minimal freight rates. Loading 7,500 tons of wheat in bags took about 14 days—no overtime, no nights, no week-end work. Occasionally we would unload on the Baltic or North European coasts. Later, when things improved, this charter was varied by, for example, sending ships to load timber in British Columbia for Australian or South African ports, or to Tampico (Mexico) to load asphalt in drums for Australia or Malaya. Another variation required loading wheat in Australia for China, whence we would proceed in ballast to the Philippines to load copra and tobacco for Italy, France and Spain. Of course, as this developed so the leisurely days of bag loading passed, and it became a frantic rush".

Ships were dry-docked once a year and even during the worst of the slump the steamers were kept in ready condition. Pride in the ships was enhanced by the manning policy, as related by the late J. Lisle, Chief Engineer, "when a man was promoted Master or Chief Engineer he remained on his ship unless moved at his own request, and this often applied to the lower officer ranks. The result was evident in the performance of the ships, which were always beautifully kept". Captain Lewis joined King Line as Third Officer on "King Stephen" in 1929, was promoted Second Officer, returned to her on promotion to Chief Officer, and after the war, during which he served on various other ships including "King Edwin" and "Empire Earl" his first ship became his first command.

By the thirties several of the older captains, some of whom had served the Company since the turn of the century, were reaching retirement. Captain "Willie" Davies, for example, of "King Howel", retired in 1929, as did Captain George Ritch, eldest of three brothers who had served King Line since 1895, who came ashore in 1927 to supervise the building and entry into service of the new motorships. The other brothers also retired about this time, Charles, the quietest of the three, and the flamboyant Magnus, one-time amateur heavyweight boxing champion of Scotland—a distinction that arguably served him at least as well in his chosen profession as did his certificate. A favourite story, probably apocryphal, of these brothers was that on one voyage, and one only, all three had served aboard the same ship—George in command. Charles and Magnus as first and second mates. The scuppers flowed non-stop with their blood throughout the voyage. Of course more than a certificate was needed to command a tramp in those days—"hard-case ships, hungry workhorses" as Captain Buller apprenticed aboard "Don Cesar" in 1909 under Captain Charles Ritch, described them, and as Captain George Smith noted "they knew their business—tough to a degree—and capable. I shall never forget their brilliant handling of the various hangers-on to authority that creep aboard in certain ports avid for "grat and jam"—and I shall always be in their debt for what I learned from them in the early twenties. They were also sincere, God-fearing men. In early 1928 when Chief Officer of "King Gruffydd" I and my Captain, R. H. (Bobby) Evans visited Magnus, he the toughest, bravest, hardest of them all, aboard "King James", where he was listening to another Captain concluding a description of a hurricane he had experienced with the words "Believe me, I went on my knees that night". Magnus at once barked out "The first time?" to which Bobby Evans added "Tell the truth, you go on your knees every night like the rest of us" and to my surprise all three confirmed that they never missed their nightly prayers, and from that day onwards neither have I." Captain Smith took command of "King Gruffydd" succeeding Captain R. H. Evans, who took over the new "King Neptune". Sail-trained Captain Evans, had achieved fame when commanding the Robert Thomas barque, "Denbigh Castle" in the early years of the century. Well over 70, and affectionately known as "old Father Neptune" he came ashore in 1937, to be succeeded by Captain John Ritch, son of George.

Newly promoted captains included Angus MacNeil, winner of one of the first military O.B.E.'s, in recognition of his work behind the Turkish lines in 1917. He was in another war to add a civil O.B.E. and retired post-war to his native Barra, a very fine man indeed, who Her Majesty specially asked to meet when she visited the island in the 1950's, after his retirement. Another newly promoted Captain was A. W. Wheeler, first appointed to "King Edgar", remaining with her until her loss in March 1945. He subsequently commanded her successor and namesake for six years, making over 21 years in two ships of the same name.

In 1933 Sir Vernon became Chairman of the Tramp Shipping Advisory Committee and handled the protracted negotiations which led to the Government granting a Tramp Shipping Subsidy, in recognition of which he was not only the subject of a House of Commons tribute from Walter (later Lord) Runciman, then President of the Board of Trade, but also awarded a Baronetcy.

A new Management Agreement was negotiated in 1934 between King Line and their managing company, reconstituted as Dodd, Thomson & Co. (1934) Ltd. on the following scale:

(a) $8\frac{1}{2}$p (previously $12\frac{1}{2}$p) per Gross Ton.
(b) 5% (previously $7\frac{1}{2}$%) Net Profit Commission on Voyages.
(c) 1% (previously $1\frac{1}{4}$%) on purchases, sales and buildings.
(d) One-third of 5% (unchanged) Freight Brokerage on Time Charter.

It will be recalled that in 1931 the managers had waived half the income to which they were entitled under the old scheme. The new agreement was to run for five years from 1934, but in fact remained in force until termination of the arrangement in 1950.

An additional responsibility assumed by Sir Vernon in 1932, was a directorship of Union Castle Mail Steamship Company, followed almost immediately by appointment as Deputy Chairman and in 1934 as Joint Managing director (with Robertson F. Gibb). Union Castle's finances had suffered heavily as a result of the association with R.M.S.P. and additionally the fleet was distinctly antiquated. By 1939 huge liabilities had been honoured, and the fleet modernised to a degree that even eclipsed Lord Kylsant's achievements with the R.M.S.P. fleet in 1903–1913, and for this much credit was due to Sir Vernon.

As the 1930's drew to their close, the tempo of activity built up again as the fleet, aided by the Subsidy, returned to full employment. Three steamers were sold in 1937–38, realising sums well in excess of their book values. Dividends were resumed, with a special bonus to mark the line's forthcoming Golden Jubilee. That landmark was scarcely passed before the fleet found itself once more at war with Germany.

Dodd Thomson & Co. Ltd. — War and Reconstruction

The first loss occurred on November 12th, 1939 when M.V. "King Egbert" was mined off the Norfolk Coast and the last on March 2nd, 1945 when her sister ship "King Edgar" was torpedoed and sunk in the North Atlantic. Betweeen these, 12 other "Kings" succumbed, leaving only 4 survivors on V.E. Day. It is a representative picture of the service given by the Merchant Marine.

The two following losses were not of ships, but of personnel. Lord Kylsant's son-in-law, the Earl of Coventry, was killed in action at Dunkirk, on May 28th, 1940. A few days later, on 12th June, George Dodd, who had been taken ill while visiting London for the 1940 A.G.M. died at the age of 78. This left only two directors, one of whom, Mr. Percy Cross, was in South Africa. His prospects of returning being remote, he consequently cabled his consent to the appointment of Mr. Robert B. Thomson, brother of Sir Vernon. Later in the year Mr. Oscar Hall was appointed a director. He had joined Philipps, Philipps and Co. Ltd in October 1911 and was elected to the Baltic Exchange in 1914 when he became Assistant Chartering Clerk to Sir Vernon.

A month later "King John" fell victim to the raider "Widder" commanded by Korvetten Kapitan von Ruckteschell, an officer black-listed by the Allies after serving in submarines during the First World War, and who subsequently drew a ten year sentence in respect of his treatment of prisoners during the Second.

"King John" had been warned of "unusual" activity on the passage chosen for her and was required to report any unusual features. The convoy dispersed after 3 days and "King John" rescued 21 officers and men of the "Santa Margarita" a Yugoslav owned vessel which had been torpedoed and sunk.

Shortly before noon on July 13th a ship was reported steaming fast to port. This ship fired one shell, narrowly missing "King John's" bow and then opened fire with all her guns as "King John" swung to starboard, one shell hitting the poop and moving the steering gear two feet. An S.O.S. was sent at 11.57 G.M.T. and, as "King John" was no longer answering her helm, the engine was stopped and the Chief Officer was ordered to get as many of the crew as possible into the port boat and pull away. Simultaneously the Second Officer reported that heavy shrapnel on the after deck and poop prevented him from returning the raider's fire. The Master, Captain George F. Smith, after dumping the "confidential" bag, went to the Radio Room while the Radio Officer, Dudley Golden, sent out his messages—despite the raider's attempts at jamming, three signals had been transmitted before the raider was able to silence transmission by bringing down the second aerial.

"King John" was in ballast and riding high out of the water. The raider maintained her fire on the upperworks, and as "King John" was soon afire amidships, navigational instruments were passed into the starboard boat and orders given to abandon ship. Captain Smith and his Chief Engineer, Mr. J. Lisle were ordered aboard the raider which had adopted the guise of the Swedish steamer "Narvik" and Captain Smith recalls "when I turned to wave good-bye to my men, I received the highest honour I have or ever will have. They cheered me". The remaining officers and survivors were left to sail 4 days to Sombrero and from there to Dog Island, where rescue eventually awaited them, and it was during this voyage that Mr. Dudley Golden drafted the report to the owners on the loss.

Mr. Lisle has been quoted as saying that the treatment accorded prisoners aboard her was "first class within the scope of a raider" but in a letter to the author he said "I read that von Ruckteschell had been sentenced to ten years for the conditions under which he kept prisoners on board. This was during his second cruise. The first was never mentioned and none of us was called. Otherwise his sentence might have been heavier. However, the men themselves weren't too bad". Captain Smith suspected that things might be difficult for himself and his reply to von Ruckteschell's comment that "She is hard to sink" of "Naturally, made in Britain" did not help. After sinking "King John" the raider made off. From Germany Captain Smith recommended both Radio Officers, who had to be ordered twice to leave the ship, for awards, while he himself discovered on his return from being "entertained" at prisoner-of-war camp and, for a spell by the Gestapo, that he had been awarded the O.B.E. and Lloyds Silver Medal.

Sir Vernon Thomson, detail from a portrait in 1950 by David Jagger R. A.   *King Line Ltd.*

"King Gruffydd" was torpedoed on 17th March 1943 in the North Atlantic whilst part of Convoy SC 122. This battle, considered by many to be a turning point in the Battle of the Atlantic, was studied in detail by Martin Middlebrook in his book "Convoy".

"King Edwin", which had previously sailed in Convoy OB 318 when U-110 commanded by Fritz-Julius Lemp of "Athenia" notoriety was captured, complete with codebooks—an event described by H.M. King George VI as perhaps the most important accomplishment in the whole war at sea—met her end in the Grand Harbour Malta on 14th April, 1943. She loaded her final cargo at Alexandria (Egypt) for Malta, 4,000 tons of Aviation Spirit in drums, ammunition, machinery and food. "King Edwin" was under the command of Captain D. J. Lewis, and his Chief Officer and Chief Engineer were J. A. Lewis and E. Ferry respectively. During discharge, which had only been in progress a few hours, there was a terrific explosion in No. 1 Hold, followed by a similar one in No. 2 and in a matter of minutes the vessel was a blazing inferno. Several lives were lost and many more were badly burnt and injured. She became a constructive total loss. After the fire had been extinguished, Lord Gort, Governor of Malta, boarded the burnt out bulk and congratulated the three senior officers. Finally, in August 1945, the wreck was raised for harbour clearance and taken out to sea on V.J. Day, and, as part of the victory celebrations, sunk in deep water by naval gunfire.

At the end of the War only the motorships "King Neptune", "King Stephen" and "King William" and the older "King James" owned by the Scottish Steamship Co. survived.

At the outbreak of War, Sir Vernon Thomson had been appointed Director of Commercial Services at the Board of Trade and, in November 1939, Principal Shipping Adviser and Controller of Commercial Shipping at the Ministry of Shipping (later Ministry of War Transport). Sir Vernon, being Chairman of both tramp and liner companies, was a particularly appropriate choice. He was also Chairman of the Merchant Shipbuilding Advisory Committee and all this work was, as the Minister, Lord Leathers, later said, of invaluable service to his country and to the War effort.

Mr. Oscar Hall was also appointed to high office in the Ministry of Shipping, commencing in Bunkering, North Atlantic. It is recalled that he was originally assisted by 6 Civil Servants. However, these gentlemen soon proved themselves so remarkably capable that they had perforce to be promoted and were replaced by two men (of Mr. Hall's choice) and a number of girl temporaries. Thus armed, he became responsible for the co-ordination of the 4,000 plus ships in "Operation Overlord" ensuring that each and every one was in the right place at the right time with the right men and equipment.

These services were recognised by the award of the O.B.E. to Mr. Hall in 1941 and the advancement to G.B.E. of Sir Vernon in 1946. An O.B.E. was offered to Mr. John S. Bevan, who had served throughout the War as Sir Vernon's personal assistant, but this honour was declined by the intended recipient.

So far as was possible the general routines of running a company were maintained as before. The greater part of the administration was transferred to the Cardiff Office, leaving only a skeleton staff in London in the charge of Mr. Cyril French, who had joined the chartering staff in 1935. Board meetings were held often at highly unconventional hours, and often at the Thomson's home in Hertfordshire. Arrangements were made in 1942 to acquire two of the diesel-engined standard ships the company were then managing on behalf of His Majesty's Government, and this decision together with the acquisition of two further vessels of like design, one diesel, the other steam propelled, was speedily implemented at the War's end, to join the surviving pre-war ships. Another decision worthy of note in 1941 was to "give £500 as a token of the board's esteem" to a former officer, retired in 1929 and evidently fallen upon hard times, there then being no Pension Fund.

The Cardiff office had long been the headquarters of the Engineer Superintendent, the first of whom was Mr. A. Walker, who held the position for over twenty years until his death early in 1940 when he was succeeded by Mr. George Rooks. Mr. Lindsay Dryden was appointed Assistant Superintendent when he came ashore from "King Neptune" in Plymouth in March 1940, after serving aboard her for eleven years. Between them these men were directly responsible for the maintenance of the fleet, hull and machinery, diesel or steam, for close on 40 years as well as supervision of tonnage under construction.

Towards the end of 1948 it was announced that the Board recommended acceptance of the offer from Union-Castle Mail Steamship Co. Ltd. (of which company Sir Vernon was also chairman) of £5 per share not already held by it, worth £2,500,000. King Line shares were at that time quoted at £3.87p. King Line however, continued to be managed as a totally separate enterprise. A second Empire-type steamer was transferred from Union-Castle, re-named "King James" and like "King Edgar" converted from coal to oil burning. Shortly afterwards, the Management Agreement with Dodd Thomson and Co. Ltd. lapsed by agreement and henceforth King Line was managed by its Board of Directors.

KING JAMES   *World Ship Photo Library*

The Union-Castle offer resulted from a decision by their Directors that their company's high-class tonnage could usefully be supplemented by additional general cargo vessels—a decision which conveniently overlooked the fact that, with Sir Vernon as Chairman of both Union-Castle and King Line, this "supplement" was in practice available anyway, and had in fact already been utilised. The offer was acceptable to King Line because Union-Castle was in 1948 financially one of the soundest concerns in the City of London, and a suitable vehicle to secure the future of the smaller but no less sound King Line. Corroboration of this came from Captain J. A. Lewis "Towards the end of 1952, when I was about to depart on a Shaw Savill charter to New Zealand, I was instructed to call upon Sir Vernon. My relationship with Sir Vernon had always been happy, although there were some who had noted that advancing years had not mellowed his sometimes volcanic temper, and it was for that reason that such instructions were known to sea-going staff as "Appointment with Fear", after a popular radio series of the time. Sir Vernon as ever, received me most cordially, and after discussing ships' business for about twenty minutes, he asked after my family, and, as he led me to the door, he shook me by the hand and said "Captain, you may wonder why I am not at the King Line office as often as I used to be. I have not forgotten you, and never shall. As you know King Line are now part of Union-Castle. I did this, knowing that when the time comes for me to cross the River, the King Line will be in good and capable hands. Goodbye and good voyage." Within a few weeks Sir Vernon had died.

One complication arose in that not only were substantial numbers of shares in King Line held by London Maritime Investment Co., of which Sir Vernon was Chairman, but furthermore, both King Line and Union-Castle had substantial holdings in London Maritime, which when combined resulted in London Maritime becoming a subsidiary of Union-Castle. The Union-Castle Directors did not deem it appropriate to have a subsidiary company not directly connected with their shipping interests, and consequently sold their interest. The sale included London Maritime's subsidiary Scottish Steamship Co., whose remaining ship "King James" laid up since 1947, was sold in 1950 and the company ceased trading.

Later that year, two open shelter deck motorships of 9,500 tons dwt. and capable of 12½ knots were ordered from Harland and Wolff Ltd. on a fixed price contract quoted at £455,000 each. An option to order a third vessel was subsequently exercised, but by then the builders felt obliged to stipulate a price variation clause, which increased the cost by £107,000.

KING ARTHUR   *World Ship Photo Library*

The occasional Union-Castle time charter apart, the fleet continued to sail world-wide. Australian grain to the U.K. and to Egypt still featured, as did timber from the north Pacific coast, phosphates from Sfax to Brazil, iron-ore from Brazil to Cardiff, coal from Calcutta to Japan, and wheat from New Orleans to Bombay, all typical fixtures reported in the halcyon years of the early fifties.

KING STEPHEN   *World Ship Photo Library*

One voyage particularly merits attention. "King Stephen", commanded by Captain A. J. MacInnes sailed with cars from Dagenham to Geelong and Sydney, then wheat from Sydney to Callao, nitrate from Jocopilla to Alexandria, wheat thence to Nagasaki where the high prices then being offered for shipping by the Japanese induced the company to offer her for sale. However, the Japanese declined to pay £280,000 in 1951, so onwards in ballast to Coos Bay, Oregon to load timber for Lourenco Marques, then coal to Aden, salt from Aden to Nagoya, and a second Pacific transit in ballast to load timber in British Columbia for Avonmouth. "Tramping at its best, 3 times round the world in 22½ months, earning £550,000 in freight. On my end-of-voyage interview with Sir Vernon his opening remark that I had had a record voyage did not surprise me."

23

Early in 1951 an episode occurred which throws an interesting light on Sir Vernon Thomson. Much has been made elsewhere during and after his life-time of his resolute teetotalism, his being a bachelor and his generally austere way of life. This story, told by Miss Axten, may help to balance the scales. "On Sir Vernon's seventieth birthday, on 10th February 1951, he gave each of us in the office a cheque for 25 guineas—which was a very large amount at that time—drawn on his own personal account, to mark the occasion, telling us that "up to the age of seventy one lives by the grace of God, but beyond that, by the special grace of God".

At the end of 1952 Mr. F. W. Matthews retired, after serving King Line as Secretary for 41 years. Responsibility for the finances of a limited company is traditionally that of the Secretary, and if credit for the Company's working has been given to others, it should not be forgotten that he too made a notable contribution over the years. Less than two months later, a sadder blow fell with the death, on February 8th 1953, of Sir Francis Vernon Thomson Bt., G.B.E. two days before his 72nd birthday. The shipping press, describing him as "one of the ablest leaders of the shipping industry" devoted columns to his obituary notices, recalling his work for tramp shipping over 55 years, and his war-time services, of which the Minister, Lord Leathers said, "A substantial share of the credit for the successful operation of the Allied shipping operation in two world wars must be apportioned to Sir Vernon". A Board Minute, on 31st March, 1953, noted "Throughout his long business life he unsparingly devoted his keen administrative powers, his sound judgement and outstanding skill in ship management to furthering the interest of the King Line. This with his unshakeable integrity, his dynamic energy and enthusiasm so happily infused into all those associated with him greatly enhanced the fortunes and prestige of the company whose reputation is now recognised as second-to-none wherever British ships trade". His place as chairman was taken by his brother, Mr. R. B. Thomson and another close colleague, Mr. J. S. Bevan of the Union-Castle Line was appointed a Director in his stead.

The King Line found themselves in the centre of a "diplomatic incident" in October 1953, when the new "King Malcolm" was in Rosario. One of her Cadets was Peter Markham, whose duties included responsibility for breaking out and lowering the ensign and the courtesy flag (the Argentine flag). He writes "Shortly after the flags were lowered one Sunday evening, the ship was boarded by the Marineros (Naval Police), who alleged that I had, when lowering the Argentine flag, thrown it on the deck, spat on it, and generally wiped the deck with it. The fact that the flag in question was new and spotless did not convince the police of their error and I was taken to their headquarters and deprived of my tie, belt, shoe-laces and the contents of my pockets. A hint that a gift of nylons, or perfume for the wife of the officer in charge might cause the matter to be dropped was not much use to an apprentice on £9 per month. I was conducted to a cell, pressed on by swipes from night-sticks and swords—to which I had the sense not to react—where I joined four other prisoners. The food and bedding was appalling, but fortunately Captain Drever, who had been ashore at the time I was arrested, arrived at 11.30 p.m. and bailed me out. However, I was re-arrested next morning and spent five days in custody, when the Justices dismissed the case against me and I was released to re-join my ship". At the time the British and Argentinian Goverments were indulging in one of their not infrequent differences of opinion, on this occasion over meat.

In 1955 orders were placed for three further motorships of the "King Malcolm" class. Later that year terms were agreed between the boards of Clan Line Steamers Ltd. and Union-Castle Mail Steamship Co. Ltd. for the merger of their interests into the British and Commonwealth Shipping Co. Ltd., of which King Line became a subsidiary. The merger took effect on January 1st, 1956 and, at the King Line board meeting on February 22nd, 1956, Mr. R. B.Thomson relinquished the position of Chairman in favour of Mr. J. S. Bevan, while Mr. Oscar Hall O.B.E., was appointed Managing Director, the first to hold the title since Lord Kylsant became Chairman in 1892.

It was also about time that George Rooks, Engineer Superintendent since 1940, died suddenly in hospital. A great-hearted and utterly loyal servant of the company, his place was taken by his Deputy, Mr. Lindsay Dryden.

The first Marine Superintendent had been appointed in 1955—Captain A. B. Drever, formerly in command of "King Malcolm" while a further point of note, this time in 1956 was the service of Mr. Oscar Hall on the Committee for landings in Egypt during their short-lived Anglo-French invasion of the Suez Canal area.

Sir Nicholas Cayzer, Bt.   *King Line Ltd.*

The Old Order Changeth, Yielding Place to New

The operations of King Line were initially scarcely affected by the formation of "British and Commonwealth Steamship Co.," and for some years the fleet continued to trade much as before despite a gradual tendency for "Kings" to sail on Clan or Union Castle berths more frequently.

The entry into service of "King Charles" and "King George" in 1957 facilitated the disposal of the veterans "King Neptune" and "King Stephen", sold for £310,000 and £260,000 respectively for further trading in the Far East. The money realised reflected great credit on the work of the Engineer Superintendents Messrs. A. Walker, G. Rooks and L. Dryden, underlined a year or so previously by the results of a survey on the ships condition carried out by Harland and Wolff, who reported to the Directors in highly complimentary terms concerning the ships' general structural and mechanical condition after over a quarter of a century's service.

There were further changes in 1958. The sudden death of Captain Drever resulted in the promotion of Captain A. J. MacInnes to Marine Superintendent, while in March of that year Mr. Lindsay Dryden, Engineer Superintendent, retired, and with his retirement the long-established Cardiff office was closed. The company also sold its last steam-powered vessels "King Edgar"in 1959 and "King James" in 1958.

"King James" departure was not regretted. Freight rates had dropped well below the level at which she could be operated profitably and she sailed under command of Captain J. A. Lewis from Middlesbrough. "Her boilers, never reliable, required constant attention, and we were always breaking down at sea. This culminated in a major refit at Nagasaki prior to delivery at Hong Kong in April 1958. One of the few times the engines were working was when a whale chose to surface dead ahead at zero range. That sprung a few rivets in the fore-peak. All in all, the happiest day of the voyage was the one when I boarded the Hunting Clan aircraft at Hong Kong, homeward bound, complete with five well-filled log books chronicling the voyage. I learnt of her eventual fate with no surprise at all".

"King Henry" entered service in December 1958, the last traditional King Line tramp and the last Group ship built at Belfast. Her cost of £921,000 was about £100,000 less than the combined cost of all eleven motor Kings bought by Lord Kylsant, the last of which "King William" went to the breakers in July 1959, still capable of 10 knots on 8 tons oil daily (laden). "King Henry" for comparison, made $12\frac{1}{2}$–13 knots on 13 tons daily, although when her tonnage openings were closed a few years later, her speed was reduced by half a knot on the same consumption. Her five half-sisters were similarly altered.

Always a popular ship, "King Henry's" maiden voyage was, like those of so many of her predecessors, coal outwards to the Plate and grain homewards. Her design had been revised so that unlike her sister-ships, she did not have No. 3 hatch between the bridge and funnel, and other modifications gave her a slightly more built-up look. Another innovation was the white superstructure and grey masts and derricks as worn by the Clan Line.

The retirements of Oscar Hall, O.B.E., Managing Director, and of Miss Alice Axten, who had held a wide variety of senior posts during her 43 years service, at the end of 1959 and 1960 respectively seemed symbolic of further changes. Mr. Hall was succeeded by Mr. Cyril French. King Line shares had already been transferred from Union Castle to the parent Company, and in place of investments sums representing inter-company balances now featured in the Balance Sheet. These increased substantially with the transfer of ownership of the six post-war motorships to other Group Companies, and the repainting of their funnels in Clan Line colours. King Line now became responsible for Group Chartering requirements and Ship Purchases and Sales, and additionally for a period, for managing the fleet of the South American Saint Line. Depressed freight rates in the early sixties led to the sale of many of the Clan Line war-built ships, most of which appeared on the King Line register in transit.

New tonnage was considered, but profitable employment remained unassured, and three ships ordered as tramps, with the suggested names "King Canute" "King Edward" and "King Harold" were eventually completed as "Clan Macgregor", "Clan Macgillivray" and "Clan Macgowan". The general surplus of shipping, depressed freight rates, and increasing pressure from India and South Africa for greater shares in their trade by their own ships led to rationalisation of the Conference routes in the early 1970's and the eventual prospect of containerisation. There followed another massive clear-out of "Clans", "Castles" and the six "Kings", the last of which, "King Charles" was delivered to her new owners in February 1973.

Meantime there had been other developments. Mr. Cyril French had retired after 30 years service, in 1965, and Mr. Bernard Jones joined King Line in his stead, with Mr. Roy Morris as Assistant Managing Director. Shortly afterwards British and Commonwealth started to consider the possibilities of the bulk cargo carrier, including a consortium operation with overseas shipowners. Eventually opportunity presented itself in 1967 when one of two vessels of 80,000 tons deadweight building at the Burmeister and Wain yard at Copenhagen was offered to the Group, and this being considered a reasonable opportunity to gain experience in this type of operation at a comparatively low outlay, the offer was accepted. The vessel, engaged on an 8 year charter to Krupps, was commissioned under the name "Elbe Ore", and placed in the

KING RICHARD

Courtesy of the owners

ownership of Scottish Tanker Co. Ltd. When the charter expired in 1975 she was renamed "King Richard"—a name new to King Line yet one of historical significance, for it was Richard I who had granted the founder's family the right to add the gold collar and chain which forms part of the Company's house flag.

Twelve months later, a second bulk carrier joined the fleet. This vessel, of 54,250 tons deadweight, had already undergone two name changes while building, but on completion was placed under King Line ownership, and, as the Company's first bulk carrier, it was appropriate that the new era should be marked by the name "King Alfred", the fourth vessel to bear the name. A third ship followed in 1970, and three more, all from Spanish yards, in 1974–1975.

Current trading prospects are not good, as the market has yet to recover from the slump in rates which started in 1974. Consequently, the giants, the largest of which each have a carrying capacity well in excess of the ten ships of the 1905 programme, or the nine motorships of 1928–1929, or the six post-war motorships, are making heavy weather, with only "King William", on a five year charter expiring late in 1979, really profitable. There is one more change. After 19 years of Clan Line colouring, the "Kings" are reverting to the original King Line livery. King Line's other activities continue. Early in 1977 the remaining "Clans" on King Line register were transferred back to Clan Line. However, containerisation of the South African route has led to further sales since 1977, and King Line has already sold "Windsor Castle" the Group's last passenger liner, and the last two Cape mailships, "Southampton Castle" and "Good Hope Castle", on behalf of Union-Castle Line.

Given an improvement in freight rates, King Line, after 90 years spent in the shadow of the R.M.S.P., of Union Castle, and of British and Commonwealth, enters its tenth decade as the largest shipowner of its Group, while the great liner companies with which it was connected through the persons of the founder, Lord Kylsant, and through Sir Vernon Thomson, will almost or entirely have passed into history.

What memories remain over the years? Two of those who have contributed so much to this short narrative have amassed between them over eighty years service. Let the last words in the Idyll of the Kings be theirs.

Captain G. F. Smith O.B.E. (1917–1963) "I cannot deny that Lord Kylsant, George Dodd, and Sir Vernon Thomson were ideal men in my eyes. The Ritch's and Bobby (Capt. R. H.) Evans exemplars truly worthy of imitation as well as admiration. Crews whose loyalty was to the ship, one was proud to lead them and serve with them. The wonderful men I met all over the world, especially in the business and academic worlds, in agreement or in opposition. God has indeed been kind and generous to this old sailor, if not in material, then in the real things that matter, mainly the many friends I made and memories that I hold".

Captain J. A. Lewis (1929-1965). "In my retirement my mind returns to those long past happy days with the Company, to the friendly people of countless Australian ports in the thirties. King Line were an entity in the shipping world and after George Dodd and Sir Vernon Thomson had passed on, they had such outstanding men and gentlemen as Oscar Hall and Cyril French. Who of the sea-going staff can forget the outstanding George Rooks, by whose untimely death the company lost a loyal and brilliant servant, and the sea-going staff a true friend; or his successor Lindsay Dryden. In my opinion King Line were the best tramp concern in the United Kingdom, and I shall always have happy recollections of my service with them".

FLEET LIST NOTES
1. Details are extracted from Lloyds Registers, amplified by information recorded in the Minute Books of King Line Ltd., Annual Accounts, and other records maintained by that Company.
2. Vessels are listed in order of acquisition by one of the companies named, and, after 1959, acquisition by one of the Ship-owning companies within the British and Commonwealth Group, viz. Clan Line, Hector Whaling Co., Houston Line, and Scottish Tanker Co.
   Inter-Company transfers are recorded as and when they took place.
3. The notation '1', '2', etc., in brackets after a ship's name indicates that she is the first, second, etc., ship of that name in the fleet. The dates following the name are those of entering and leaving the fleet.
   On the first line is given the ship's Official Number (ON.) in the British registry [where allocated] followed by her tonnages gross ('g'), nett ('n') and deadweight ('d'), and her dimensions. Deadweight tonnages of vessels built prior to 1930 are approximate. Minor variations in tonnage measurements during a ship's career have been ignored. Dimensions of ships completed up to 1952 are the registered dimensions — length between perpendiculars x breadth x moulded depth – in feet and tenths of a foot. From 1952 onwards the details given are length overall x breadth x loaded draught in feet and inches. All measurements have been expressed in Imperial measures.
   On the second line is given the type of engines, and the name of the engine builders. 'T.3-cyl.' = triple expansion three cylinder steam engines. 'Q4-cyl' = quadruple expansion four cylinder steam engines. The figures which follow are the diameter of the cylinders and the length of stroke of the piston in inches together with the indicated horse power (ihp). For motor vessels, the number of cylinders is given and whether they are two stroke cycle (2SC.) or four stroke cycle (4SC) and whether single acting (SA.) or double acting (DA.). The brake horse power (bhp) is also quoted where available.
4. The ship's histories are corrected to December 1979.

FLEET LIST
Section I.
King Line Ltd. and connected companies.
VESSELS OWNED BY KING LINE, SCOTTISH STEAMSHIP CO. AND BRITISH MOTORSHIP CO. MANAGERS 1889–1923: PHILIPPS, PHILIPPS & CO. LTD, 1923–1950: DODD, THOMSON & CO. LTD.

1. KING ALFRED (1) (1889–1894)
ON. 96086. 1189g, 769n, 923d. 225.0 × 32.7 × 15.8 feet
T.3-cyl: 16½".27".44"–33". 99nhp by North Eastern Marine Engineering Co. Ltd., Newcastle.
9.1889: Completed by The Blyth Shipbuilding Co. Ltd., Blyth for King Alfred Steamship Co. Ltd.
1893: Owners' style changed to King Line Ltd. *4.4.1894:* Wrecked on South Uist whilst on a voyage from Fernandina, Florida, to Bo'ness with phosphates.

2. KING BLEDDYN (1) (1894–1902)
ON. 102663. 2351g, 1479n, 3350d. 285.0 × 41.0 × 17.8 feet
T.3-cyl: 21".35".57"–39". 1000ihp by Blair & Co. Ltd., Stockton.
2.1894: Completed by Robert Thompson & Sons, Sunderland, for King Line Ltd. *1902:* Sold to J. Th. Sifneo, Russia and renamed ELENI JEAN SIFNEO under Greek flag. *1905:* Sold to E. Vlassopoulo, Greece and renamed ANARGYROS SIMOPOULOS. *5.3.1909:* Sank after striking a shoal off Imbros whilst on a voyage from Kustendie to Naples with grain.

3. KING ARTHUR (1) (1894–1899)
ON. 99172. 1229g, 772n, 231.5×32.5×13.4 feet
T.3-cyl: 16½".26".44"–33". 109nhp by Central Marine Engine Works, West Hartlepool.
7.1891: Completed by Robert Irvine & Co., West Hartlepool as SILVIA for J. Sutcliffe, Grimsby.
1894: Purchased by King Line Ltd., and renamed KING ARTHUR. *1899:* Sold to P. D. Darcourt, France and renamed GYPTIS. *1903:* Sold to Charles Scholl, France, name unchanged. *1923:* Sold to Marcel Goossens, Belgium, name unchanged. *28.11.1924:* Wrecked at Point Coubre whilst on a voyage from Cardiff to Bordeaux with coal.

4. KING CADWALLON (1) (1894–1898)
ON. 99049. 2380g, 1530n, 3520d. 289.6 × 39.1 × 19.1 feet
T.3-cyl: 21".35".57"–39". 1000ihp by Blair & Co. Ltd., Stockton.
3.1892: Completed by The Blyth Shipbuilding Co. Ltd., Blyth as AURIGA for Oriental Steamship Co. Ltd., London. *1894:* Purchased by King Line Ltd., and renamed KING CADWALLON. *1898:* Sold to Sota y Aznar, Spain and renamed BAKIO. *26.1.1902:* Stranded on the North Pier, Hook of Holland, whilst on a voyage from Rotterdam to Cardiff in ballast, and sank.

SAC SANTANDER at Barcelona 22.4.63 awaiting demolition   *Raul Maya collection*

5. KING DAVID (1). (1895–1905)
ON. 105743. 2555g, 1530n, 4100d. 304.0×44.1×20.6 feet
T.3-cyl: 23".37½".67½"–39". 1200ihp by Blair & Co. Ltd., Stockton. 9k.
10.1895: Completed by Short Brothers, Sunderland for King Line Ltd. *1905:* Sold to Cia Avilesina de Nav., Spain and renamed ACUARIO. *1906:* Transferred to Honduras registry. (M. Carreno manager). Subsequently reverted to Spanish registry. *1907:* Transferred to Uruguayan registry. (F. de Carcamo manager). *1911:* Sold to Fabregas y Garcias, Spain and renamed TERESA PAMIES. *1924:* Owners became P. Garcias Segui, Spain. *1932:* Sold to Soc. Anon Cros, Spain, and renamed SAC 9. Owners style subsequently changed to Transportes Aduanas y Consignaciones S.A. *1950:* Renamed SAC SANTANDER. *1963:* Sold for breaking up at Barcelona.

6. KING EDGAR (1) (1896–1901)
ON. 105807. 2552g, 1610n, 4200d. 304.1 x 44.1 x 20.6 feet
T.3-cyl: 23".37½".67½"–39". 1200ihp by Blair & Co. Ltd., Stockton. 9k.
3.1896: Completed by Short Brothers, Sunderland for the Scottish Steamship Co. Ltd. *1901:* Sold to Cia. Estrella (Prado y Torres, managers), Spain and renamed ELORRIO. *1905:* Owners' style changed to Cia. de Naviera La Estrella (Juan L. Prado, manager). *1917:* Sold to Cia. de Naviera Begona (J. M. Urquijo, manager), Spain and renamed BEGONA No. 1. *1919:* Sold to L. Ibran, Spain and renamed SANTOFIRME. *1927:* Sold to V. Figaredo Herrero, Spain. *1931:* Renamed VICENTE FIGAREDO. *1934:* Broken up.

7. KING FREDERICK (1) (1897–1905)
ON. 108216. 2577g, 1550n, 4200d. 310.4 x 44.1 x 20.3 feet
T.3-cyl: 23".37½".67½"–39". 1200ihp by Blair & Co. Ltd., Stockton. 9k.
6.1897: Completed by Short Brothers, Sunderland for King Line Ltd. *1906:* Sold to Cia Avilesina de Nav. (M. Carreno, manager), Honduras and renamed LEO. *26.4.1907:* Lost in collision off Finisterre whilst on a voyage from Garrucha to the Clyde with iron ore.

8. KING GRUFFYDD (1) (1898–1906)
ON. 108382. 2994g, 1934n, 5100d. 324.8 x 48.6 x 21.3 feet
T.3-cyl: 24".40".65"–42". 1400ihp by Kincaid & Co. Greenock. 9k.
7.1898: Completed by Russell & Co., Port Glasgow for King Line Ltd. *1906:* Sold to Bank of Athens (A. M. Coulouthros, manager), Greece and renamed MICHAEL. *7.6.1908:* Lost in collision off Lisbon whilst on a voyage from Cardiff to Genoa with coal.

9. MEXICANO (1902–1903) Tanker
ON. 98781. 1973g, 1264n. 270.0 x 38.2 x 22.6 feet
T.3-cyl: 21".35".57"–39". 1000ihp by Westgarth, English & Co., Middlesbrough.
1893: Completed by J. Laing, Sunderland for R. Craggs & Sons, Middlesbrough. *1895:* Sold to Northern Transport Ltd. (Petersen, Tate & Co., managers), Newcastle. Name unchanged. *1900:* Management transferred to Philipps, Philipps & Co. Ltd., *1902:* Purchased by King Line Ltd. Name unchanged. *16.9.1903:* Foundered in the Atlantic during a hurricane after heavy seas flooded the stokehold and extinguished the boiler fires, whilst on a voyage from Philadelphia to Vera Cruz with a cargo of petroleum.

BARNSTABLE   *Peabody Museum of Salem*

10. BARNSTABLE (1902–1913)
ON. 98782. 1356g, 745n, 900d. 230.2 x 31.5 x 15.0 feet
T.3-cyl: 22".35".57"–36". 1050ihp by Westgarth, English & Co. Middlesbrough. 13k.
3.1894: Completed by R. Craggs & Sons, Middlesbrough, for their own account. *1895:* Sold to Northern Transport Ltd. (Petersen, Tate & Co., managers), Newcastle. Name unchanged. *1900:* Management transferred to Philipps, Philipps & Co. Ltd., *1902:* Purchased by King Line Ltd. Name unchanged. *4.1913:* Sold to T. W. Ward Ltd., for demolition at Briton Ferry.

11. BROOKLINE (1902–1913)

ON. 98783. 1356g, 745n, 900d. 230.2 × 31.5 × 22.2 feet
T.3-cyl: 22".35".57"–36". 1050ihp by Westgarth, English & Co., Middlesbrough. 13k.
4.1894: Completed by R. Craggs & Sons, Middlesbrough, for their own account. *1895:* Sold to Northern Transport Ltd. (Petersen, Tate & Co., managers), Newcastle. Name unchanged. *1900:* Management transferred to Philipps, Philipps & Co. Ltd., *1902:* Purchased by King Line Ltd. Name unchanged. *4.1913:* Sold to T. W. Ward Ltd., for demolition at Morecambe.

KING CADWALLON aground   *Raul Maya collection*

12. KING CADWALLON (2) (1904–1906)

ON. 113915. 3275g, 2126n. 326.2 × 48.1 × 23.8 feet
T.3-cyl: 24".40".65"–42". 1400ihp by the Shipbuilders. 9k.
10.1900: Completed by A. Rodger & Co., Port Glasgow as EDDERTON for McLaren and McLaren, Glasgow. *1904:* Purchased by King Line Ltd. and renamed KING CADWALLON. *22.7.1906:* Grounded on Lewis Rocks, St. Martin's Island, Scillies, whilst on a voyage from Barry to Naples with coal, and subsequently sank in deep water.

13. KING ARTHUR (2) (1905–1912)

ON. 120514. 3968g, 2589n, 6410d. 340.7 × 47.1 × 20.0 feet
T.3-cyl: 25".41".67"–45". 1700ihp by Blair & Co. Ltd., Stockton. 9k.
4.1905: Completed by R. Stephenson & Co. Ltd., Newcastle for the Scottish Steamship Co. Ltd. *1906:* Transferred to King Line Ltd. *5.1912:* Stranded and subsequently refloated. *1912:* Sold to Cia. Commercio e Nav., Brazil and renamed MERITY. *1915:* Sold to A/S D/S Hassel (A/S Rederiet Odfjell, managers), Norway and renamed HASSEL. *1929:* Sold to Kristiansunds Nye Rederi A/S (H. Schnitler Ltd. A/S managers), Norway and renamed MAIZE. *1934:* Sold for breaking up in the U.K.

KING BLEDDYN   *World Ship Photo Library*

14. KING BLEDDYN (2) (1905–1916)

ON. 120623. 4387g, 2853n, 7380d. 355.0 × 50.1 × 27.4 feet
T.3-cyl: 26".43".70"–45". 1750ihp by the Shipbuilders. 9k.
10.1905: Completed by Palmers' Shipbuilding and Iron Co. Ltd., Newcastle for King Line Ltd.
1.12.1916: Captured by UC21 and scuttled by bombs 30 miles S by W½W of Ushant, in position 47.54N 05.07W, whilst on a voyage from New York to Havre with a cargo of steel, copper and shell cases.

KING EDWARD
Raul Maya collection

15. KING EDWARD (1) (1906–1924)

ON.120671. 4357g, 2832n, 7270d. 355.4 × 50.1 × 27.6 feet
T.3-cyl: 26".42½". 69½"–45". 1750ihp by Blair & Co. Ltd., Stockton. 9k.
2.1906: Completed by R. Stephenson & Co. Ltd., Newcastle for King Line Ltd. *1924:* Sold to Redcroft S.N. Co. (1921) Ltd. Cardiff and renamed MARCHIONESS OF BUTE. *1925:* Lewis Lougher & Co. Ltd. appointed managers. *1926:* Owners' style changed to Redcroft S.N. Co. Ltd., same managers. *9.1932:* Sold for breaking up in Italy. *3.11.1932:* Arrived at Savona for demolition by Ardito S.A.

MARCHIONESS OF BUTE, note upper bridge
World Ship Photo Library

16. KING DAVID (2) (1906–1917)

ON. 106510. 3680g, 2360n, 6150d. 350.0 × 50.1 × 23.3 feet
T.3-cyl: 25".41".67"–45". 1700ihp by Blair & Co. Ltd., Stockton. 9k.
5.1906: Completed by Craig, Taylor & Co. Ltd., Stockton for King Line Ltd. *10.7.1917:* Captured by U49 and sunk by gunfire 360 miles NW½W Fastnet.
Note: A model of this vessel may be seen in the Neptune Hall, National Maritime Museum, Greenwich.

17. KING FREDERICK (2) (1906–1917)
ON.119225. 3756g, 2397n, 6150d. 350.4 x 50.1 x 23.1 feet
T.3-cyl: 25".41".67"–45". 1700ihp by North Eastern Marine Engineering Co. Ltd., Sunderland. 9k.
5.1906: Completed by Short Brothers Ltd., Sunderland for King Line Ltd. *1915:* Sold to G. C.
Dracoulis, Greece and renamed NIRITOS. *12.4.1917:* Sunk with explosive charges by the Austrian
submarine U27, 5 miles from Augusta, Sicily.

18. KING IDWAL (1) (1906–1917)
ON.119903. 3631g, 2321n, 6150d. 350.5 x 50.1 x 23.2 feet
T.3-cyl: 25".41".67"–45". 1700ihp by the Shipbuilders. 9k.
9.1906: Completed by J. Readhead & Sons, South Shields for King Line Ltd. *22.11.1917:*
Torpedoed and sunk by U boat 29 miles SE by E½E from Buchan Ness.

KING HOWEL   *Captain A. R. Williamson*

19. KING HOWEL (1) (1906–1916)
ON. 123701. 4343g, 2822n, 7250d. 355.2 x 50.1 x 27.5 feet
T.3-cyl: 26".43".70"–45". 1750ihp by Palmers' Shipbuilding & Iron Co. Ltd., Newcastle. 9k.
9.1906: Completed by R. Stephenson & Co. Ltd., Newcastle for King Line Ltd. *1916:* Sold to The
Bay S.S. Co. Ltd., London and renamed BAYHOWEL. *1921:* Sold to Soc. Anon. de Nav. "Les
Armateurs" Francaise, France and renamed HOHNECK. *1922:* Sold to G. Macris, Greece and
renamed ARTEMISSIA. *1935:* Sold to M. A. Tachmindji, Greece and renamed ALEXANDROS.
15.9.1940: Torpedoed and sunk by U48 in a position 56.50N 15.04W.

20. KING JOHN (1) (1906–1919)
ON. 124272. 3644g, 2352n, 6152d. 350.0 x 50.2 x 23.2 feet
T.3-cyl: 25".41".67"–45". 1700ihp by Blair & Co. Ltd., Stockton. 9k.
10.1906: Completed by J. L. Thompson & Sons Ltd., Sunderland for King Line Ltd. *1919:* Sold to
James McKelvie, London and renamed CARLO VICTORIA. *1920:* Sold to A and C Aboaf Ltd.,
London. Name unchanged. *1923:* Sold to Soc. Paulista de Nav. Matarazzo Ltda., Brazil and
renamed LYDIA M. *1952:* Sold to Luciano Castro y Cia Ltda., Brazil and renamed ANTONIO
CASTRO. *1956:* Sold to Nav. Santista Ltda., Brazil. Name unchanged. *1962:* Sold to Domingos
Goncalves Martins, Brazil. Name unchanged. *16.2.1970:* Suffered fire in her boiler room whilst on
a voyage from Paranagua to Macau in ballast. The vessel was declared a constructive total loss
and broken up at Rio de Janeiro, by Irmaos Almeida who began work in 9.1970.

21. KING LUD (1) (1906–1914)
ON. 124273. 3650g, 2344n, 6150d. 350.0 x 50.3 x 23.2 feet
T.3-cyl: 25".41".67"–45". 1700ihp by Blair & Co. Ltd., Stockton. 9k.
11.1906: Completed by J. L. Thompson & Sons Ltd., Sunderland for King Line Ltd. *25.9.1914:*
Whilst on a voyage from Alexandria to Calcutta in ballast, captured 25 miles SSW Point de Galle,
in position 05.45N, 80.00E by the German cruiser EMDEN and sunk by bombs.

KING LUD *Raul Maya collection*

22. KING MALCOLM (1) (1906–1916)

ON. 123744. 4351g, 2829n, 7250d. 355.2 × 50.1 × 27.5 feet
T.3-cyl: 26".43".70"–45". 1750ihp by Palmers' Shipbuilding & Iron Co. Ltd., Newcastle. 9k.
11.1906: Completed by R. Stephenson & Co. Ltd., Newcastle for the Scottish Steamship Co. Ltd.
28.11.1916: Torpedoed and sunk by U39, 144 miles NW by N of Alexandria in a position 33.14N,
28.23E, whilst on a voyage from Marseilles to Mauritius in ballast.

23. KING ARTHUR (3) (1912–1913)

ON.119976. 2848g, 1792n. 314.0 × 48.0 × 20.6 feet
T.3-cyl: 23".38".62"–42". 1200ihp by North Eastern Marine Engineering Co. Ltd., Sunderland. 9k.
9.1905: Completed by Sunderland Shipbuilding Co. Ltd., as KINGSLAND for Kingsland Steamship
Co. Ltd. (S. R. Ruston & Co., managers), Cardiff. *1909:* Management transferred to Philipps,
Philipps & Co. Ltd. *1912:* Purchased by the Scottish Steamship Co. Ltd., and renamed KING
ARTHUR. *1913:* Sold to J. L. Mowinckel, Norway and renamed HEINA. *1920:* Transferred to J.
Ludwig Mowinckels Rederi, Norway. *1921:* Sold to Reiersen & Matland, Norway and renamed
STRUDSHOLM. *1921:* Sold to M. Sato, Japan. *1922:* Renamed ATSUTA MARU No. 1. *1924:*
Owners' style changed to Sato Shokai Goshi Kaisha. *27.8.1926:* Wrecked at Tsuchizaki.

KING ALFRED *Alex Duncan*

24. KING ALFRED (2) (1919–1940)

ON. 137268. 5275g, 3195n, 8380d. 400.0 × 52.4 × 28.5 feet
T.3-cyl: 27".44".73"–48". 2500ihp by the Shipbuilders. 11k.
26.6.1919: Launched by Wm. Doxford & Sons Ltd., Sunderland as WAR AZALEA ("A" Type), for the Shipping Controller, His Majesty's Government. *1919:* Purchased by King Line Ltd., and in *9.1919* completed as KING ALFRED. *4.8.1940:* Torpedoed by U52 in a position 56.59N, 17.38W whilst on a voyage from Halifax to Liverpool. She broke in two and the bow section sank. The stern section was later sunk by gunfire from His Majesty's ships.

KING BLEDDYN   *World Ship Photo Library*

25. KING BLEDDYN (3) (1920-1937)

ON.142726. 6498g, 4040n, 10,760d. 412.4 × 55.8 × 34.4 feet
T.3-cyl: 27".44".73"–48". 2500ihp by the Shipbuilders. 10k.
12.1918: Completed by Harland & Wolff Ltd., Belfast, as WAR MUSIC for the Shipping Controller, His Majesty's Government (Clyde Shipping Co. Ltd., managers). *1919:* Sold to Glen Line Ltd., London and renamed GLENSPEY. *4.1920:* Purchased by King Line Ltd., and renamed KING BLEDDYN. *1937:* Sold to Halcyon-Lijn NV, Netherlands and renamed STAD MAASSLUIS. *1950:* Sold to Francescu Pittaluga fu Giacomo, Italy and renamed FRANCESCU. *6.4.1954:* Stranded off Bats in the Schelde estuary whilst on a voyage from Bona to Antwerp with a cargo of iron ore. Broke in two and became a total loss.

26. KING DAVID (3) (1921–1938)

ON. 143147. 3721g, 2257n, 6077d. 355.1 × 50.4 × 23.2 feet
T.3-cyl: $25\frac{1}{2}$".$41\frac{1}{2}$".$67\frac{1}{2}$"–$47\frac{1}{2}$". 1900ihp by the Shipbuilders. 9k.
9.1912: Completed by A. G. Weser, Bremen as GUNDOMAR for Hamburg Bremer-Afrika Linie A.G. Germany. *1919:* Ceded to Shipping Controller, His Majesty's Government (Lamport & Holt Line Ltd., managers). *1921:* Purchased by King Line Ltd., and renamed KING DAVID. *12.1938:* Sold to Capt. O. E. Bertin, Shanghai (French flag) and renamed HORTENSIA BERTIN. [Gross tonnage now 4764]. *1941:* Sold to Panamanian Freighters (Wallem & Co., managers), Panama and renamed NICARAGUA. *1946:* Sold to Shanghai Development Co. Ltd., China and renamed GREATER SHANGHAI. *1950:* Sold to Far Eastern and Panama Transport Corporation (Wheelock Marden & Co. Ltd., managers). Panama and renamed MIRAMAR. *1951:* Ownership taken over by the Government of the People's Republic of China and renamed HOPING ERR. *1962:* Deleted from "Lloyd's Register" owing to absence of recent information.

KING GRUFFYDD   *Captain G. F. Smith*

27. KING GRUFFYDD (2) (1923–1943)
ON. 147512. 5063g, 3145n, 8050d. 400.9 × 52.4 × 28.3 feet
T.3-cyl: 27".44".73"–48". 2500ihp by the Shipbuilders. 11k.
11.10.1919: Launched by Hong Kong and Whampoa Dock Co. Ltd., Hong Kong as WAR TROOPER
for the Shipping Controller, His Majesty's Government. *1919:* Sold to N. E. Ambatielos, Greece
and *12.1919:* Completed as AMBATIELOS. *6.1923:* Auctioned by order of the Admiralty Marshal
following dispute with the owner who failed to take delivery, and bought by King Line Ltd.
Renamed KING GRUFFYDD. *17.3.1943:* Torpedoed and sunk by U338 in a position 51.55N,
32.41W, whilst on a voyage from New York to Hull.

KING CADWALLON gutted and aground   *Alex Duncan*

28. KING CADWALLON (3) (1923–1929)
ON. 151412. 5063g, 3145n, 8050d. 400.9 × 52.4 × 28.3 feet
T.3-cyl: 27".44".73"–48". 2500ihp by the Shipbuilders (fitted to burn oil fuel). 11k.
3.1920: Launched by Hong Kong and Whampoa Dock Co. Ltd., Hong Kong as WAR PIPER for the
Shipping Controller, His Majesty's Government. *1920:* Sold to N. E. Ambatielos, Greece. *7.1920:*
Completed as STATHIS. The owner failed to take delivery and in *1921:* Reverted to the Shipping
Controller (Glover Brothers, managers). *6.1923:* Auctioned by order of the Admiralty Marshal and
purchased by King Line Ltd. Renamed KING CADWALLON. *7.7.1929:* Caught fire in a position
32.01S, 40.41E SE of Durban whilst on a voyage from Methil to Melbourne with coal. *12.7.1929:*
Ship abandoned. *20.8.1929:* Wreck salvaged and towed to East London. *12.9.1929:* Wreck broke
free and grounded during storm.

29. KING FREDERICK (3) (1923–1944)
ON. 146631. 5106g, 3165n, 8100d. 400.2 × 52.3 × 28.5 feet
T.3-cyl: 27".44".73"–48". 2500ihp by the Shipbuilders. 11k.
12.1919: Launched by Hong Kong and Whampoa Dock Co. Ltd., Hong Kong as WAR SCEPTRE for
the Shipping Controller, His Majesty's Government. *1920:* Sold to N. E. Ambatielos, Greece.
3.1920: Completed as TRIALOS. The owner failed to take delivery and *1922:* Reverted to the
Shipping Controller (Glover Brothers, managers). *6.1923:* Auctioned by order of the Admiralty
Marshal and bought by King Line Ltd. Renamed KING FREDERICK. *4.7.1940:* Damaged in air
attack in the English Channel but repaired. *19.7.1944:* Torpedoed and sunk by U181 in a position
09.29N, 71.45E whilst on a voyage from Haifa to Calcutta.

KING FREDERICK *World Ship Photo Library*

30. KING HOWEL (2) (1923–1937)
ON. 147506. 5102g, 3168n, 8270d. 400.2 × 52.3 × 28.5 feet
T.3-cyl: 27".44".73"–48". 2500ihp by the Shipbuilders. 11k.
16.8.1919: Launched by Taikoo Dockyard and Engineering Co. of Hong Kong Ltd., Hong Kong as
WAR MINER for the Shipping Controller, His Majesty's Government. *1919:* Sold to N. E.
Ambatielos, Greece. *10.1919:* Completed as STATHIS. *1920:* Renamed CEPHALONIA. *6.1923:*
Auctioned by order of the Admiralty Marshal following dispute with the owner who failed to take
delivery, and bought by King Line Ltd. Renamed KING HOWEL. *4.1937:* Sold to Bank Line Ltd. (A.
Weir & Co., managers) and renamed ROWANBANK. *31.1.1941:* Sunk by air attack 300 miles NW
of Ireland, in position 57.00N, 16.30W, whilst on a voyage from Freetown to Immingham.

31. KING IDWAL (2) (1923–1940)
ON. 147537. 5115g, 3164n, 8150d. 400.2 × 52.3 × 28.5 feet
T.3-cyl: 27".33".73"–48" .2500ihp by the Shipbuilders (fitted to burn oil fuel). 11k.
2.1920: Launched by Taikoo Dockyard and Engineering Co. of Hong Kong Ltd., Hong Kong as
WAR CORONET for the Shipping Controller, His Majesty's Government. *1920:* Sold to N. E.
Ambatielos, Greece. *5.1920:* Completed as KERAMIES. *6.1923:* Auctioned by order of Admiralty
Marshal following dispute with the owner who failed to take delivery, and bought by King Line Ltd.
Renamed KING IDWAL. *23.11.1940:* Torpedoed and sunk by U123 in a position 56.44N, 19.13W
whilst on a voyage from Liverpool to Baltimore.

KING EDWARD *Alex Duncan*

32. KING EDWARD (2) (1924–1942)

ON. 141921. 5217g, 3152n, 8300d. 400.0 × 52.3 × 28.4 feet
T.3-cyl: 27".44".73"–48". 2500ihp by the Shipbuilders. 11k.
26.8.1919: Launched by Workman Clark & Co. Ltd., Belfast as WAR TERRIER for the Shipping Controller, His Majesty's Government. Sold to British India Steam Navigation Co. Ltd while fitting out and *9.1919:* Completed as GORALA. *7.1924:* Bought by King Line Ltd., and renamed KING EDWARD. *27.12.1942:* Torpedoed and sunk by U156 in a position 47.25N, 25.20W.

KING JAMES, note the corrugated hull   *Captain A. J. MacInnes*

33. KING JAMES (1) (1925–1950)

ON.148705. 5066g, 3129n, 9401d. 400.3 × 59.0 × 25.9 feet
6-cyl: 4SC. SA oil engine. 1850bhp by Harland & Wolff Ltd., Glasgow. 10k.
Ordered from D. & W. Henderson & Co. Ltd., Glasgow by Petersen & Co., London and originally to be named RIVER OTTAWA. Sold on the stocks to British Motorship Co. Ltd. *11.1925:* Completed as KING JAMES. *1935:* Ownership transferred to the Scottish Steamship Co. Ltd. *1949:* Laid-up pending repairs. *1950:* Sold to Constantin Atychides (Union Maritime & Shipping Co. Ltd., managers), Liberia and renamed SOPHOCLYVE. *1954:* Transferred to Compania Oceanica de Transportes S.A. (Union Maritime & Shipping Co. Ltd., managers), Liberia. *8.8.1960:* Sank after springing a leak and being abandoned in a position 15.57N, 56.09E whilst on passage from Mormugao to Holland with a cargo of ore.

KING MALCOLM   *Alex Duncan*

34. KING MALCOLM (2) (1925–1941)

ON. 148713. 5064g, 3128n, 9401d. 400.3 × 59.0 × 25.9 feet
6-cyl: 4SC. SA oil engine. 1850bhp by Harland & Wolff Ltd., Glasgow. 10k.
Ordered from D. & W. Henderson & Co. Ltd., Glasgow by Petersen & Co., London and originally to be named RIVER ST. LAWRENCE. Sold on the stocks to British Motorship Co. Ltd. *12.1925:* Completed as KING MALCOLM. *1935:* Ownership transferred to the Scottish Steamship Co. Ltd. *31.10.1941:* Torpedoed and sunk by U374 in position 47.40N, 51.15W whilst on a voyage from Haifa to Belfast and Garston via Table Bay and Sydney N.S., with a cargo of potash.

KING ROBERT   *Alex Duncan*

35. KING ROBERT (1) (1926–1941)
ON. 148731. 5886g, 3615n, 9171d. 400.0 × 53.0 × 32.8 feet
T.3-cyl: 27".45".75"–51". 2600ihp by Richardsons, Westgarth & Co. Ltd., Middlesbrough. 11k.
11.1920: Completed by Furness Shipbuilding Co. Ltd., Haverton Hill-on-Tees, as CITTA DI MESSINA for Peirce Bros., Italy, having been ordered by Sicula Americana S.N. Co., Italy. *1926:* Purchased by the Scottish Steamship Co. Ltd., and renamed KING ROBERT. *29.1.1941:* Torpedoed and sunk by U93 in position 56.00N, 15.23W.

36. KING EDGAR (2) (1927–1945)
ON. 149947. 4536g, 2694n, 8211d. 400.6 × 54.8 × 23.6 feet
6-cyl: 4SC. SA oil engine. 1850bhp by the Shipbuilders. 10k.
11.1927: Completed by Harland & Wolff Ltd., Belfast for King Line Ltd. *2.3.1945:* Torpedoed and sunk by U1302 in a position 52.05N, 05.42W.

KING EDGAR   *Alex Duncan*

KING EDWIN   *Captain G. F. Smith*

37. KING EDWIN (1927–1943)
ON. 149964. 4536g, 2692n, 8211d. 400.6 × 54.8 × 23.6 feet
6-cyl: 4SC. SA oil engine. 1850bhp by the Shipbuilders. 10k.
12.1927: Completed by Harland & Wolff Ltd., Belfast for King Line Ltd. *16.4.1943:* Caught fire whilst unloading petrol and ammunition in Grand Harbour, Valletta, Malta, G.C., and scuttled to avoid explosion. Declared a constructive total loss. *16.1.1944:* Wreck struck by S.S. EMPIRE TRAVELLER. *6.4.1945:* Wreck raised and subsequently towed out to sea and sunk.

38. KING EGBERT (1928–1939)
ON. 149979. 4535g, 2694n, 8211d. 400.6 × 54.8 × 23.6 feet
6-cyl: 4SC. SA. oil engine. 1850bhp by the Shipbuilders. 10k.
1.1928: Completed by Harland & Wolff Ltd., Belfast for King Line Ltd. *12.11.1939:* Mined and sunk 4 miles SW of Haisbro' Lightvessel, Norfolk.

KING JOHN   *World Ship Photo Library*

39. KING JOHN (2) (1928–1940)
ON. 160356. 5228g, 3139n, 8330d. 400.7 × 54.8 × 27.2 feet
6-cyl: 4SC. SA. oil engine. 1850bhp by the Shipbuilders. 10k.
2.1928: Completed by Harland & Wolff Ltd., Belfast for King Line Ltd. *13.7.1940:* Sunk by gunfire from the German raider WIDDER in a position 20N, 60W.

40. KING LUD (2) (1928–1942)
ON. 160380. 5224g, 3136n, 8330d. 400.7 × 54.8 × 27.2 feet
6-cyl: 4SC. SA. oil engine. 1850bhp by the Shipbuilders. 10k.
3.1928: Completed by Harland & Wolff Ltd., Belfast for King Line Ltd. *8.6.1942:* Torpedoed and sunk by the Japanese submarine I-10 in a position 20S, 40E approximately, whilst on a voyage from New York to Bombay via Table Bay, with a cargo of Government stores.

KING LUD *Alex Duncan*

41. KING NEPTUNE (1928–1957)
ON. 160404. 5224g, 3136n, 8330d. 400.7 × 54.8 × 27.2 feet
6-cyl: 4SC. SA. oil engine. 1850bhp by the Shipbuilders. 10k.
4.1928: Completed by Harland & Wolff Ltd., Belfast for King Line Ltd. *1957:* Sold to Chip Hwa Shipping & Trading Co. Ltd., Singapore, and renamed WING ON. *1959:* Transferred to Hong Kong registry. *1962:* Sold to Hwa Aun (Hong Kong) Ltd. (Chip Hwa Shipping & Trading Co. Ltd., managers). *1963:* Sold to Transportes Dorados S.A., Panama. *15.8.1968:* Arrived at Kaohsiung to be broken up.

KING NEPTUNE *Captain G. F. Smith*

42. KING ARTHUR (4) (1928–1942)
ON. 160458. 5228g, 3139n, 8330d. 400.7 × 54.8 × 27.2 feet
6-cyl: 4SC. SA. oil engine. 1850bhp by the Shipbuilders. 10k.
5.1928: Completed by Harland & Wolff Ltd., Belfast for King Line Ltd. *15.11.1942.* Torpedoed and sunk by U67 in a position 10.30N, 59.50W.

43. KING STEPHEN (1928–1957)
ON. 160496. 5274g, 3171n, 8330d. 400.7 × 54.8 × 27.2 feet
6-cyl: 4SC. SA. oil engine. 1850bhp by the Shipbuilders. 10k.
6.1928: Completed by Harland & Wolff Ltd., Belfast for King Line Ltd. *1957:* Sold to Vanguard Shipping Co. Ltd. (World-Wide Shipping Co. Ltd., managers), Hong Kong and renamed GOLDEN DELTA. *1962:* Sold to The Corinthian Shipping Co. Ltd. (World-Wide Shipping Co. Ltd., managers), Hong Kong. *1965:* Sold to Fuji Marden & Co. Ltd. who commenced demolition at Hong Kong *4.3.1965.*

KING WILLIAM   *World Ship Photo Library*

44. KING WILLIAM (1) (1928–1959)
ON. 160516. 5274g, 3171n, 8330d. 400.7 × 54.8 × 27.2 feet
6-cyl: 4SC. SA. oil engine 1850bhp by the Shipbuilders. 10k.
7.1928: Completed by Harland & Wolff Ltd., Belfast for King Line Ltd. *7.1959:* Sold to Hanwa Co. Ltd., Tokyo for breaking up.

45. KING ALFRED (3) (1945–1963)
ON. 167003. 6919g, 4151n, 9750d. 432.2 × 56.2 × 33.2 feet
4-cyl: 2SC. SA oil engine 2500bhp by Barclay Curle & Co. Ltd., Glasgow. 11k.
1941: Completed by Greenock Dockyard Co. Ltd., as EMPIRE RAY for Ministry of War Transport (James Chambers & Co., managers). *1944:* Management transferred to Dodd, Thomson & Co. Ltd. *9.1945:* Purchased by King Line Ltd., and renamed KING ALFRED. *18.11.1962:* Laid up in the River Blackwater. *1963:* Sold through Eckhardt & Co., Hamburg to Eisen und Metall A. G., Hamburg and arrived there *16.3.1963* for breaking up.

KING DAVID   *Alex Duncan*

46. KING DAVID (4) (1945–1962)
ON. 168664. 7251g, 4352n, 10437d. 427.0 × 56.5 × 35.5 feet
3-cyl: 2SC. SA. oil engine. 2500bhp by the Shipbuilders. 11k.
3.1941: Completed by Wm. Doxford & Sons Ltd., Sunderland as EMPIRE MIST for Ministry of War Transport (Haldin & Philipps Ltd., managers). *1943:* Management transferred to Dodd, Thomson & Co. Ltd. *11.1945:* Purchased by King Line Ltd., and renamed KING DAVID. *1962:* Sold to Pan Norse Steamship Co. S.A., Liberia and renamed HONG KONG VENTURE. *1966:* Sold to Unity Carriers Inc. (Wah Kwong & Co. (Hong Kong) Ltd., managers), Liberia. *19.4.1969:* Arrived at Hong Kong to be broken up by Ming Hing.

KING EDGAR   *World Ship Photo Library*

47. KING EDGAR (3) (1946–1959)
ON. 169444. 7084g, 4335n, 10070d. 432.2 × 56.3 × 34.3 feet
T.3-cyl: $24\frac{1}{2}''.39''.70''-48''$. 2500ihp by the Shipbuilders. $10\frac{1}{2}$k.
1945: Completed by Harland & Wolff Ltd., Glasgow as EMPIRE GAMBIA for Ministry of War Transport (Moller Line (U.K.) Ltd., managers), and almost immediately sold to King Line Ltd. *1946:* Renamed KING EDGAR. *1959:* Sold to Iwai & Co. Ltd., for breaking up. *18.5.1959:* Demolition began at Osaka.

KING ROBERT   *World Ship Photo Library*

48. KING ROBERT (2) (1946–1961)
ON. 168522. 6981g, 4164n, 9630d. 432.9 × 56.3 × 34.3 feet
6-cyl: 4SC. SA. oil engine. 2500bhp by Harland & Wolff Ltd., Glasgow. $11\frac{1}{2}$k.
3.1943: Completed by Harland & Wolff Ltd., Belfast as EMPIRE GRANGE for Ministry of War Transport (Sir R. Ropner & Co. Ltd., managers). *1946:* Purchased by King Line Ltd., and renamed KING ROBERT. *5.1961:* Sold to Mullion & Co. Ltd., Hong Kong and renamed ARDGEM. *1967:* Sold to Kelso Shipping Co. Ltd., Gibraltar and renamed KELSO. *2.9.1969:* Arrived at Kaohsiung to be broken up.

49. KING JAMES (2) (1950–1958)
ON. 180051. 7067g, 4879n, 10080d. 431.0 × 56.3 × 35.2 feet
T.3-cyl: $24\frac{1}{2}''.39''.70''-48''$. 2500ihp by J. Dickinson & Sons Ltd., Sunderland. 10k.
13.12.1943: Completed by Short Brothers Ltd., Sunderland as EMPIRE DUCHESS for Ministry of War Transport (H. Hogarth & Sons Ltd., managers). *7.8.1946:* Management transferred to the Union-Castle Mail Steamship Co. Ltd. *1949:* Sold to the Union-Castle Mail Steamship Co. Ltd., and renamed BRAEMAR CASTLE. *1950:* Purchased by King Line Ltd., and renamed KING JAMES. *1958:* Sold to Cambay Prince S.S. Co. Ltd. (John Manners & Co. Ltd., managers), Hong Kong and renamed TYNE BREEZE. *1963:* Sold to Cathay Trader Steamship Co. Ltd., Hong Kong and renamed CATHAY TRADER. *1964:* Sold to the Pacific Pearl Nav. Co. Ltd., Hong Kong and renamed PEARL LIGHT. *1966:* Sold to Marikar Navigation and Agencies Ltd., Hong Kong and renamed HARIB MARIKAR. *3.11.1967:* Suffered an engine breakdown whilst on passage from Hong Kong to Chittagong and later grounded on Lincoln Island in position 16.30N, 112.50E, becoming a total loss.

KING MALCOLM   *Alex Duncan*

50. KING MALCOLM (3) (1952–1972)
ON. 184575. 5883g 3386n, 9535d. 466'6"×59'2"×25'9"
6-cyl: 4SC. SA. oil engine. 3300bhp by the Shipbuilders. 12½k.
2.1952: Completed by Harland & Wolff Ltd., Belfast for King Line Ltd. *12.1959:* Transferred to The Clan Line Steamers Ltd. *1.1963:* Transferred to Hector Whaling Ltd. *6.1972:* Sold to Soloi Compania Naviera S.A. (Alassia Steamship Co. Ltd., managers), Cyprus and renamed KANARIS. Still in service.

KING ALEXANDER   *World Ship Photo Library*

51 KING ALEXANDER (1952–1972)
ON. 184628. 5883g, 3346n, 9510d. 466'6"×59'2"×25'9"
6-cyl: 4SC. SA. oil engine. 3300bhp by the Shipbuilders. 12½k.
5.1952: Completed by Harland & Wolff Ltd., Belfast for King Line Ltd. *12.1959:* Transferred to The Clan Line Steamers Ltd. *1.1963:* Transferred to Hector Whaling Ltd. *9.1972:* Sold to Ilyssia Compania Naviera S.A. (Alassia Steamship Co. Ltd., managers), Cyprus and renamed ELLI 2. Still in service.

52. KING ARTHUR (5) (1953–1972)
ON. 185856. 5883g, 3346n, 9570d. 466'6"×59'2"×25'9"
6-cyl: 4SC. SA. oil engine. 3300bhp by the Shipbuilders. 12½k.
3.1953: Completed by Harland & Wolff Ltd., Belfast for King Line Ltd. *11.1959:* Transferred to The Clan Line Steamers Ltd. *1.1963:* Transferred to King Line Ltd. *5.1972:* Sold to Kition Compania Naviera S.A. (Alassia Steamship Co. Ltd., managers), Cyprus and renamed TOULLA. Still in service.

KING CHARLES   *World Ship Photo Library*

53. KING CHARLES (1) (1957–1973)
ON. 187593. 5737g, 3242n, 9506d. 466'6"×59'2"×25'9"
6-cyl: 4SC. SA. oil engine 3300bhp by the Shipbuilders. 12½k.
6.1957: Completed by Harland & Wolff Ltd., Belfast for King Line Ltd. *11.1959:* Transferred to The Clan Line Steamers Ltd. *1970:* Transferred to Houston Line Ltd. *2.1973:* Sold to Cephissos Shipping Co. Ltd (Aegis Shipping Co. Ltd., managers), Cyprus and renamed AEGIS MIGHT. *1976:* Sold to Marmari Shipping Corporation Ltd., Greece (same managers). *1979:* Sold to Taiwan Shipbreakers and *27.7.1979:* Arrived at Kaohsiung for demolition.

54. KING GEORGE (1) (1957–1972)
ON. 187694. 5732g, 3303n, 9607d. 466'6"×59'2"×25'9"
6-cyl: 4SC. SA. oil engine. 3300bhp by the Shipbuilders. 12½k.
12.1957: Completed by Harland & Wolff Ltd., Belfast for King Line Ltd. *12.1959:* Transferred to The Clan Line Steamers Ltd. *1970:* Transferred to Houston Line Ltd. *11.1972:* Sold to Lemythou Compania Naviera S.A. (Alassia Steamship Co. Ltd., managers), Cyprus and renamed ELENI 2. Still in service.

KING GEORGE   *World Ship Photo Library*

KING HENRY   *Captain G. F. Smith*

55. KING HENRY (1958–1972)
ON. 300806. 5829g, 3229n, 9523d. 466'6"×59'2"×25'9"
6-cyl: 4SC. SA. oil engine. 3300bhp by the Shipbuilders. 12½k.
12.1958: Completed by Harland & Wolff Ltd., Belfast for King Line Ltd. *10.1959:* Transferred to
The Clan Line Steamers Ltd. *1970:* Transferred to Houston Line Ltd. *11.1972:* Sold to Grandmar
Compania Naviera S.A. (A. Marcopoulos, manager), Greece and renamed AFRICAN LION. Still in
service.

KING ALFRED   *Courtesy of the owners*

56. KING ALFRED (4) (1968–   ) Bulk Carrier
ON. 335920. 29419g, 22033n, 54250d. 713'10"×97'2"×42'0"
8-cyl: 2SC. SA. oil engine. 12000bhp by the Shipbuilders. 15½k.
2.4.1968: Launched by Eriksbergs M/V A/B, Gothenburg as ANGELUS for I/S Angelus (H. Angel
Olsen, managers), Norway. Sold whilst fitting out to Olsen & Ugelstad A/S, Norway and renamed
HEMSEFJELL. Whilst still fitting out purchased and in *9.1968:* Completed as KING ALFRED for
King Line Ltd. *1977:* Transferred to Houston Line Ltd. In the present fleet.

57. KING JAMES (3) (1970–1978) Bulk Carrier
ON. 339322. 30289g, 20462n, 52558d. 678'8"×95'4"×43'7"
6-cyl: 2SC. SA. oil engine, 15000bhp by Astilleros Espanoles S.A., Sestao. 16k.
21.2.1970: Launched by Astilleros Espanoles S.A., Matagorda as ARALAR for Naviera Artola S.A.,
Spain. Purchased whilst fitting out and in *10.1970:* Completed as KING JAMES for King Line Ltd.
7.1978: Sold to Gwarnek & Co. Liberia and renamed NUMBER FOUR. Still in service.

KING JAMES *Courtesy of the owners*

KING WILLIAM in Clan Line colours *Courtesy of the owners*

58. KING WILLIAM (2) (1974–   ) Bulk Carrier
ON. 363134. 44146g, 31318n, 78238d. 840'7"×105'11"×47'4"
9-cyl: 2SC. SA. oil engine. 23200bhp by the Shipbuilders. 16k.
2.1974: Completed by Astilleros Espanoles S.A., Sestao for King Line Ltd. *1977:* Transferred to
The Scottish Tanker Co. Ltd. In the present fleet.

KING CHARLES   *Courtesy of the owners*

59. KING CHARLES (2) (1974–   ) Bulk Carrier
ON. 363376. 30276g, 20454n, 53399d. 678'4"×95'4"×43'7"
6-cyl: 2SC. SA. oil engine. 15000bhp by Astilleros Espanoles S.A., Bilbao. 16k.
7.1974: Completed by Astilleros Espanoles S.A., Matagorda for King Line Ltd. In the present fleet.

60. KING RICHARD (1975–   ) Bulk Carrier
ON.309977.42725g, 30919n, 77800d. 817'7"×105'9"×47'0"
8-cyl: 2SC. SA. oil engine. 16800bhp by the Shipbuilders. 15k.
25.11.1966: Launched by Burmeister & Wain, Copenhagen as ELBE ORE for Transatlantic Bulk Carriers Inc. (Krupp Reederei, managers), Liberia. *1967:* Whilst fitting out, purchased by Scottish Tanker Co. Ltd., and chartered to Krupps. Name unchanged. *1974:* Transferred to King Line Ltd., and renamed KING RICHARD. *1978:* Transferred to The Scottish Tanker Co. Ltd. In the present fleet.

61. KING GEORGE (2) (1975–   ) Bulk Carrier
ON. 363563.43742g, 32109n, 78239d, 840'7"×105'11"×47'4"
9-cyl: 2SC SA. oil engine. 23200bhp by the Shipbuilders. 15¾k.
2.1975: Completed by Astilleros Espanoles S.A., Sestao for King Line Ltd. In the present fleet.

KING GEORGE   *Builders' photograph*

SECTION II.

During the period 1961-1977 certain vessels originally registered with 5 other Group companies (excluding Union-Castle) were transferred into King Line ownership for varying periods.

"Kinpurnie Castle" and "Kinnaird Castle" were originally built for Clan Line, and, following a brief period under the South African flag, were repurchased and given "Castle" names in 1962. At no time were they ever registered with Union-Castle.

Trading Vessels

Name	Yr. Built	Gross Tonnage	King Line Ownership
Clan Ferguson	1962	9022	1962-1965
Clan Macgregor	1962	9039	1962-1963; 1969-1977
*Clan Macgowan	1963	9039	1963; 1969-1970
*Kinpurnie Castle	1954	8121	1966-1968
*Kinnaird Castle	1956	7718	1968-1975
Clan Graham	1962	9142	1969-1977
Clan Grant	1962	9142	1969-1976
Clan Macgillivray	1962	9039	1962-63; 1969-1977

*Sold out of the Group when leaving King Line ownership

Vessels owned on completion and/or pending Sale.

Name	Yr. Built	King Line ownership	Name	Yr. Built	King Line ownership
Clan Macbrayne	1942	1961	Clan Farquharson	1962	1962; 1968
Clan Allan	1942	1961	Clan Finlay	1962;	1962; 1968
Clan Lamont	1939	1961	Clan Forbes	1962	1968
Clan Davidson	1943	1961	Clan Maclennan	1947	1971
Clan Campbell	1943	1961	Clan Maclachlan	1947	1971
Clan Mackellar	1944	1961	Clan Mactavish	1949	1971
Clan Mackinnon	1945	1961	Clan Mactaggart	1949	1971
Clan Murdoch			Clan Sutherland	1951	1971
(ex Hesperia)	1946	1962	Clan Macintyre	1952	1976
Clan Chattan	1944	1962	Clan Maclay	1947	1976
Clan Chisholm	1944	1962			
Clan Brodie	1941	1962-63			

3. In 1973 two tankers of the STAT 55 design were ordered from Cammell Laird Shipbuilders Ltd., Birkenhead by King Line Ltd., and were given "Scottish" names as had previous tankers owned by Group Companies.

B.I. SCOTTISH LION (1979-   ) Tanker
ON 386247. 32995g. 21625n., 56490d. 687' 9" × 105' 11" × 40'0".
6-cyl. 2S.C.S.A. oil engine. 17400 bhp by G. Clark & N.E.M. Ltd., Wallsend. 16½k.
7.1979: Completed by Cammell Laird Shipbuilders Ltd., Birkenhead for King Line Ltd. In the present fleet.

B.2 SCOTTISH EAGLE (1980-   ) Tanker
13.7.1979: Launched by Cammell Laird and due for delivery in 1980. Sister ship to SCOTTISH LION.

1. VESSELS MANAGED BY PHILIPPS, PHILIPPS AND CO. LTD IMMEDIATELY FOLLOWING THE END OF THE 1914–1918 WAR ARE LISTED WITH THE LETTER 'C' PRECEDING THE FLEET NUMBER.

2. VESSELS MANAGED BY DODD, THOMSON AND CO. LTD. DURING AND AFTER THE 1939–1945 WAR ARE LISTED WITH THE LETTER 'D' PRECEDING THE FLEET NUMBER.

3. VESSELS OWNED BY THE BUENOS AIRES AND PACIFIC RAILWAY CO. LTD. (MANAGED BY GEO. DODD AND CO.) FROM 1906–1918 ARE LISTED WITH THE LETTER 'E' PRECEDING THE FLEET NUMBER.

C1. ISIS (1919–1921)
ON. 143133. 8833g, 5564n. 476.6 × 62.4 × 34.9 feet
T.3-cyl: 29.9".48.8".80.7"–55.1". 483nhp by the Shipbuilders.
1915: Completed by J. C. Tecklenborg A.G., Geestemunde as ISIS for Deutsche Dampfschifffahrts Gesellschaft "Kosmos" Germany. *1919:* Taken over as reparations by Great Britain and registered in the ownership of the Shipping Controller (Philipps, Philipps & Co. Ltd., managers). *1921:* Sold to David S.S. Co. Ltd., London and renamed MALVOLIO. *1921:* Sold to Vereenigde Nederlandsche Scheepvaart Maatschappij Holland and renamed AAGTEKERK. *1932:* Sold to Japanese shipbreakers.

C2. TANNENBERG (1919–1921)
ON. 143357. 7680g, 4790n. 483.2 × 62.7 × 29.7 feet
Q.4-cyl: 29.9".39.7".61.4".85"–55.1". 513nhp by the Shipbuilders.
8.1916: Completed by Bremer Vulkan Schiffbau und Maschinenfabrik Vegesack as TANNENBERG for Deutsch-Australische Dampfschiffs-Gesellschaft, Germany. *1919:* Taken over as reparations by Great Britain and registered in the ownership of the Shipping Controller (Philipps, Philipps & Co. Ltd., managers). *1921:* Sold to David S.S. Co. Ltd., London and renamed ARDOVER. *1921:* Sold to Koninklijke Nederlandsche Stoomboot Maatschappij, Holland and renamed AMERSFOORT. *20.9.1927:* Wrecked on Spanish Point, Barbuda Island, West Indies, whilst on voyage from Hamburg to Chile with general cargo.

C3. FORST (1919–1921)
ON. 143366. 5931g, 3658n. 451.4 × 58.2 × 30.9 feet
Q.4-cyl: 28.5".40".57.5".82.5"–54" 500nhp by the Shipbuilders.
1918: Completed by Flensburger Schiffsbau Gesellschaft, Flensburg as FORST for Deutsch-Australische Dampfschiffs-Gesellschaft, Germany. *1919:* Surrendered as a prize to Great Britain, registered in the ownership of the Shipping Controller (G. Dodd & Co., managers). *30.4.1921:* Purchased by Hogarth Shipping Co. Ltd. (H. Hogarth & Sons, managers), Glasgow and renamed BARON OGILVY. *1924:* Sold to Roland-Linie A.G., Germany and renamed MURLA. *1925:* Owners became Norddeutscher Lloyd, Germany. *1932:* Sold to U.S.S.R. and renamed MINSK. *1960:* Deleted from Lloyd's Register owing to lack of current information.

C4. GERA (1919–1921)
ON. 143107. 7847g, 4890n. 476.2 × 60.7 × 32.9 feet
T.3-cyl: 32.3".52.8".86.6"–55". 554nhp by the Shipbuilders.
1915: Completed by Bremer Vulkan Schiffbau und Maschinenfabrik, Vegesack as GERA for Norddeutscher Lloyd, Germany. *1919:* Surrendered as a prize to Great Britain, registered in the ownership of the Shipping Controller (Philipps, Philipps & Co. Ltd., managers). *1921:* Sold to David S.S. Co. Ltd., London. *1921:* Sold to Vereenigde Nederlandsche Scheepvaart Maatschappij, Holland and renamed OUDERKERK. *1934:* Sold to Soc. Anon, Compagnia Italiana Trasporti Marittimi Italy and renamed GIANFRANCO. *12.1941:* Seized by the Argentine Government (Flota Mercante del Estado), and renamed RIO SALADO. *1955:* Sold and broken up locally.

D1. EMPIRE COMET (1941–1942)
ON. 166996. 6914g, 4162n. 432.7 × 56.2 × 34.3 feet
6-cyl: 4SC. SA. oil engine by J. G. Kincaid & Co. Ltd., Greenock.
2.1941: Completed by Lithgows Ltd., Port Glasgow for the Ministry of War Transport (Dodd, Thomson & Co. Ltd., managers). *17.2.1942:* Torpedoed and sunk by U136 in the North Atlantic, in a position 58.15N, 17.10W. She had become detached from convoy HX174 on *9.2.1942* whilst on a voyage from Halifax N.S. to Manchester. Her captain and crew of 35 were all lost.

D2. EMPIRE LATIMER (1941–1942)
ON. 169004. 7244g, 5099n, 10340d. 428.8 × 56.5 × 35.5 feet
3-cyl: 2SC. SA. oil engine by the Shipbuilders.
12.1941: Completed by Wm. Doxford & Sons Ltd., Sunderland for the Ministry of War Transport
(Dodd, Thomson & Co. Ltd., managers). *1942:* Sold to Den Norske Stat (Norwegian Government),
(The Norwegian Shipping and Trade Mission, managers), and renamed KRONPRINSESSEN. *1946:*
Sold to A/S Kristiansands Tankrederi (Einar Rasmussen, manager), Norway and renamed
POLYTRADER. *1962:* Sold to Loucas G. Matsas and Charalambos L. Matsas, Greece. Renamed
FLORA M. *1965:* Sold to Marenviado Cia. Nav. S.A., Liberia. Name unchanged. *1968:* Sold to
Nichimen & Co. Ltd., for scrapping. *27.12.1968:* Arrived at Mihara where Seibu Kogyo K.K. began
demolition *6.1.1969.*

D3. OCEAN CRUSADER (1942)
7178g, 4280n. 425.1 × 57.0 × 34.8 feet
T.3-cyl: $24\frac{1}{2}''.37''.40''–48''$ by Canadian Allis-Chalmers Ltd., Lachine, Quebec.
11.1942: Completed by Todd-Bath Iron S.B. Corp., Portland, Maine for the Ministry of War
Transport (Dodd, Thomson & Co. Ltd., managers). *13.11.1942:* Sailed from Portland, Maine, for
Avonmouth. She called at New York, sailing from there in convoy *19.11.1942* with general cargo.
During heavy weather on *25.11.1942* she became separated from the convoy in approx. position
50N, 47W. The following day she sent out a submarine distress signal from position 50.30N,
45.30W. She had been torpedoed by U262 and sank with the loss of all hands.

D4. FORT FRANKLIN (1942–1943)
7135g, 4244n. 424.6 × 57.2 × 34.9 feet
T.3-cyl: $24\frac{1}{2}''.37''.70''–48''$ by John Inglis Co. Ltd., Toronto, Ontario.
12.1942: Completed by West Coast Shipbuilders Ltd., Vancouver B.C., for the United States War
Shipping Administration and bareboat-chartered to the Ministry of War Transport (Dodd, Thomson
& Co. Ltd., managers). *16.7.1943:* Torpedoed and sunk by U181 in the Indian Ocean between
Madagascar and Reunion, in position 22.36S, 51.22E. 5 members of her crew were killed.

D5. EMPIRE MIST (1943–1945)
See No. 46 KING DAVID.

D6. FORT NASHWAAK (1943–1947)
ON. 168428. 7134g, 4244n. 424.6 × 57.2 × 34.9 feet
T.3-cyl: $27\frac{1}{2}.''37''.70''–48''$ by Dominion Engineering Works Ltd., Montreal.
2.1943: Completed by Burrard Dry Dock Co. Ltd., Vancouver B.C. for the United States War
Shipping Administration and bareboat chartered to the Ministry of War Transport (Dodd, Thomson
& Co. Ltd., managers). *1947:* Returned to the United States Maritime Commission. *1948:* Sold to
Compania Uruguaya de Comercio y Maritima S.A., Uruguay and renamed GENERAL ARTIGAS.
1950: Sold to Oceanic Transport Corporation, Liberia. Name unchanged. *22.8.1967:* Arrived at
Kaohsiung to be broken up by Nan Tai Industry Co. Ltd.

D7. EMPIRE BOMBARDIER (1943–1944) Tanker
ON.168521. 8202g, 4781n, 465.6 × 59.5 × 33.8 feet
8-cyl: 4SC. SA. oil engine by the Shipbuilders.
2.1943: Completed by Harland & Wolff Ltd., Belfast for the Ministry of War Transport (Dodd,
Thomson & Co. Ltd., managers), having been launched as EMPIRE FUSILIER. *1944:* Management
transferred to British Tanker Co. Ltd., London. *1946:* Sold to British Tanker Co. Ltd., and renamed
BRITISH BOMBARDIER. *1959:* Sold and broken up at Tamise, Belgium by Jos Boel et fils who
began work *23.3.1959.*

D8. FORT AKLAVIK (1943–1946)
ON. 168441. 7132g, 4244n. 424.6 × 57.2 × 34.9 feet
T.3-cyl: $24\frac{1}{2}''.37''.70''–48''$ by Dominion Engineering Works Ltd., Montreal
3.1943: Completed by Burrard Dry Dock Co. Ltd., Vancouver B.C., for the Dominion of Canada and
bareboat chartered to the Ministry of War Transport (Dodd, Thomson & Co. Ltd., managers). *1946:*
Management transferred to Novocastria Shipping Co. Ltd., Newcastle. *1950:* Sold to Dalhousie
Steam & Motorship Co. Ltd., London and renamed IRENE DAL. *1952:* Sold to Compania Maritima
Volcan S.A., Panama and renamed VOLCAN. *1953:* Sold to Trans Oceanic S.S. Co. Ltd., Karachi
(Pakistan) and renamed OCEAN ENVOY. *1966:* Sold for breaking up to M. M. Bakshi who began
work in *11.1966* at Karachi.

D9. EMPIRE BENEFIT (1943–1944) Tanker
ON.168523. 8202g, 4781n. 465.6 × 59.5 × 33.8 feet
6-cyl: 4SC. SA. oil engine by Harland & Wolff Ltd., Glasgow.
4.1943: Completed by Harland & Wolff Ltd., Belfast for the Ministry of War Transport (Dodd,
Thomson & Co. Ltd., managers). *1944:* Management transferred to Athel Line Ltd, London. *1945:*
Sold to Athel Line Ltd., and renamed ATHELQUEEN. *1955:* Sold to Mariblanca Navegacion S.A.,
Liberia and renamed MARIVERDA. *1961:* Sold to Japanese shipbreakers and *6.9.1961* arrived at
Kure to be broken up.

D10. FORT CARILLON (1943–1946)
ON. 168482. 7129, 4244n. 424.6 × 57.2 × 34.9 feet
T.3-cyl: 24½".37".70"–48" by the Dominion Engineering Works Ltd., Montreal.
5.1943: Completed by Davie Shipbuilding & Repairing Co. Ltd., Lauzon, P.Q. for the Dominion of
Canada and bareboat chartered to the Ministry of War Transport (Dodd, Thomson & Co. Ltd.,
managers). *1946:* Management transferred to Union-Castle Mail S.S. Co. Ltd., London. *1949:*
Management transferred to Maclay and McIntyre Ltd., Glasgow. *1950:* Sold to Fort Carillon
Shipping Co. Ltd. (J. P. Hadoulis Ltd., managers), London and renamed MOUNT ROYAL. *1957:*
Sold to Callao Compania Naviera S.A., Liberia and renamed MONTE RICO. *1960:* Transferred to
Greek registry and renamed LAMYRIS. *1963:* Sold to Stamle Compania Naviera S.A., Greece and
renamed BARBARINO. *8.1.1968:* Ran aground off Novorissisk, U.S.S.R. in ballast and abandoned
as a total loss.

D11. FORT ST. REGIS (1943–1946)
ON. 169594. 7140g, 4240n. 424.7 × 57.2 × 34.9 feet
T.3-cyl: 24½".37".70"–48" by Dominion Engineering Works Ltd., Montreal
6.1943: Completed by Marine Industries Ltd., Sorel, P.Q., for the Dominion of Canada and
bareboat chartered to the Ministry of War Transport (Dodd, Thomson & Co. Ltd., managers). *1946:*
Management transferred to South American Saint Line Ltd. *1948:* Sold to Vancouver Oriental Line
Ltd., Vancouver and renamed YALE COUNTY *1950:* Counties Ship Management Co. Ltd.,
London, appointed managers and port of registry transferred to London. Renamed SUDBURY
HILL, *1964:* Transferred to Tower Steamship Co. (Bermuda) Ltd. (Counties Shipping Ltd.,
managers). *2.7.1967:* Arrived at Kaohsiung to be broken up.

D12. EMPIRE HOUSMAN (1943–1944)
ON. 180049. 7359g, 5017n. 431.0 × 56.5 × 35.5 feet
3-cyl: 2SC. SA. oil engine by the Shipbuilders.
12.1943: Completed by Wm. Doxford & Sons Ltd., Sunderland for Ministry of War Transport
(Dodd, Thomson & Co. Ltd., managers). *31.12.1943:* Torpedoed and damaged in the North
Atlantic, in position 60.30N, 24.35W by U545. *3.1.1944:* Torpedoed again in position 60.50N,
22.07W by U744. *5.1.1944:* Sank.

KING ALFRED   *Alex Duncan*

D13. EMPIRE RAY (1944–1945)
See No. 45 KING ALFRED.

D14. EMPIRE EARL (1944–1945)
ON. 180132. 7359g, 5008n. 431.0 × 56.5 × 35.5 feet
3-cyl: 2SC. SA. oil engine by the Shipbuilders.
5.1944: Completed by Wm. Doxford & Sons Ltd., Sunderland for the Ministry of War Transport
(Dodd, Thomson & Co. Ltd., managers). *1945:* Sold to Court Line Ltd. (Haldin & Philipps Ltd.,
managers), London and renamed CRESSINGTON COURT. *1947:* Transferred to United British S.S.
Co. Ltd., same managers. *1948:* Managers re-styled Haldin & Co. Ltd. *1952:* Transferred to Court
Line Ltd., same managers. *1958:* Sold to West Wales S.S. Co. Ltd. (Gibbs & Co. (Ship
Management) Ltd., managers), Newport and renamed EAST WALES. *1966:* Sold to Dalkeith
Shipping Co. Ltd. (International S.S. Co. Ltd., managers) Hong Kong and renamed UNIVERSAL
SKIPPER. *25.8.1970:* Delivered at Whampoa for demolition in the People's Republic of China.

D15. SAMGLORY (1944–1946)
ON. 180544. 7210g, 4389n. 423.1 × 57.1 × 34.8 feet
T.3-cyl: $24\frac{1}{2}$".37".70"–48" by Ellicott Machinery Corporation, Baltimore, Maryland.
5.1944: Completed by Bethlehem Fairfield Shipyard Inc., Baltimore for the United States War
Shipping Administration and bareboat chartered to the Ministry of War Transport (Dodd, Thomson
& Co. Ltd., managers). *1946:* Sold to Strick Line Ltd. (F. C. Strick & Co. Ltd., managers), London.
1947: Renamed SERBISTAN. *1962:* Sold to Compania de Naviera Surava S.A., Liberia and
renamed CALYPSO. *1968:* Sold to Panamic Shipping Co. S.A., Liberia. *30.3.1969:* Arrived at
Hong Kong for demolition by Leung Yau Shipbreaking Co.

D16. EMPIRE TAVOY (1945)
ON. 180150. 7381g, 4993n. 431.0 × 56.5 × 35.5 feet
3-cyl: 2SC. SA. oil engine by the Shipbuilders.
2.1945: Completed by Wm. Doxford & Sons Ltd., Sunderland for the Ministry of War Transport
(Dodd, Thomson & Co. Ltd., managers). *1945:* Sold to Leeds Shipping Co. Ltd (Sir Wm. Reardon
Smith & Sons Ltd., managers), Cardiff. *1946:* Renamed GREAT CITY. *1964:* Sold to Taiship Co.
Ltd., Hong Kong and renamed SHIPWIND. *1968:* Sold to Southern Shipping & Enterprises Co. Ltd.,
Hong Kong and renamed WING KWONG. *1969:* Sold to Wing Shun-Po (Southern Shipping &
Enterprises Co. Ltd., managers), Somali Republic. *15.1.1975:* Arrived at Shanghai to be broken up
in the People's Republic of China.

D17. EMPIRE ANTIGUA (1946)
ON. 169207. 7331g, 5172n. 431.2 × 56.3 × 35.6 feet
T.3-cyl: $24\frac{1}{2}$".37".70"–48" by J. Dickinson & Sons Ltd., Sunderland.
2.1946: Completed by Shipbuilding Corporation Ltd. (Tyne Branch), Newcastle for the Ministry of
Transport (Dodd, Thomson & Co. Ltd., managers). *1946:* Sold to The South Georgia Co. Ltd. (Chr.
Salvesen & Co., managers), Leith and renamed CULROSS. *1960:* Sold to Cia. Naviera y de
Comercio Apolo Ltda., Lebanon and renamed AKASTOS. *1962:* Transferred to Greek registry.
1966: Sold to Agenor Shipping Co. Ltd. (Aegis Shipping Co. Ltd., managers), Cyprus. *1968:* Sold
to Blue X Transocean Co. Ltd., Cyprus and renamed MARINA. *4.8.1968:* Arrived at Hamburg to be
scrapped by Eisen und Metall A.G.

E1. DON ARTURO (1906–1917)
ON. 120680. 3680g, 2360n, 6100d. 350.0 × 50.1 × 23.3 feet
T.3-cyl: 25".41".67"–45". 1700ihp by Blair & Co. Ltd., Stockton. 9k.
3.1906: Completed by Craig, Taylor & Co. Ltd., Stockton for the Buenos Aires and Pacific Railway
Co. Ltd. (George Dodd, manager), London. *28.6.1917:* Torpedoed and sunk by UC-62 during a
voyage in ballast from Algeria to the River Tees. Her entire crew of 34 was lost.

E2. DON BENITO (1906–1917)
ON. 123636. 3749g, 2395n, 6100d. 350.4 × 50.1 × 23.1 feet
T.3-cyl: 25".41".67"–45". 1700ihp by Blair & Co. Ltd., Stockton. 9k.
4.1906: Completed by Short Brothers Ltd., Sunderland for the Buenos Aires and Pacific Railway
Co. Ltd. (George Dodd, manager), London. *27.3.1917:* Sank 2 miles off Bishop's Light following a
collision with the British steamer ULTONIA (10402/98) whilst on a voyage from Swansea to
Leghorn with a cargo of patent fuel and tubes.

DON CESAR as EVERONIKA in 1939   *Raul Maya collection*

E3. DON CESAR (1906–1918)
ON. 123655. 3655g, 2343n, 6100d. 350.0 x 50.3 x 23.2 feet
T.3-cyl: 25".41".67"–45". 1700ihp by Blair & Co. Ltd., Stockton. 9k.
6.1906: Completed by J. L. Thompson & Sons Ltd., Sunderland for the Buenos Aires and Pacific Railway Co. Ltd. (George Dodd, manager), London. *1918:* Sold to Romney S.S. Co. Ltd. (Fawcett, Coverdale & Co., managers), London and renamed APSLEY. *1925:* Sold to Britain S.S. Co. Ltd. (Watts, Watts & Co. Ltd., managers), London and renamed TOTTENHAM. *1930:* Sold to Fricis Grauds, Latvia and renamed EVERONIKA. *1932:* Owners became F. Grauds Shipping Co. Ltd. *1935:* Sold to Z. Heinrichsons (F. Grauds Shipping Co. Ltd., managers), Latvia. Name unchanged. *1937:* Reverted to F. Grauds Shipping Co. Ltd. *1938:* Sold to Mrs. Elsa Grauds, Latvia, name unchanged. *1941:* Seized by the Germans when Latvia was occupied, renamed IRMA and placed under the management of H. Vogemann. *13.3.1944:* Wrecked at Vetterbae while carrying a cargo of iron ore.

E4. DON DIEGO (1906–1917)
ON. 123681. 3632g, 2321n, 6100d. 350.0 x 50.1 x 23.2 feet
T.3-cyl: 25".41".67"–45". 1700ihp by the Shipbuilders. 9k.
7.1906: Completed by J. Readhead & Sons, South Shields for the Buenos Aires and Pacific Railway Co. Ltd. (George Dodd, manager), London. *21.5.1917:* Captured by U65 40 miles E by S from Linosa, and sunk by gunfire.

E5. DON EMILIO (1906–1917)
ON. 123732. 3651g, 2345n, 6100d. 350.2 x 50.2 x 23.2 feet
T.3-cyl: 25".41".67"–45". 1700ihp by Blair & Co. Ltd., Stockton. 9k.
10.1906: Completed by J. L. Thompson & Sons Ltd., Sunderland for the Buenos Aires and Pacific Railway Co. Ltd. (George Dodd, manager), London. *1.7.1917:* Torpedoed and sunk by U80 10 miles NW by W from Esha Ness, West Scotland.

APPENDIX B
INSTRUCTIONS TO MASTERS (circa 1906)

Dear Sir,

It is understood that in accepting the command of our s.s. . . . .

. . . . you agree to hold yourself responsible for any loss or damage that may arise to the Steamer or her Owners from your neglect or in attention to any of the following Rules or Orders:—

1. be most careful with your Ship in all circumstances, and act always as if uninsured. Remember that you are legally the Agent of your Owners for all things necessary for the due fulfilment of the voyage, and responsible for the seaworthiness of your vessel (and repairs to keep seaworthy) before leaving any Port during the voyage. Before sailing be sure that your Steamer is properly loaded and stable, efficiently manned and equipped, fitted with warps, sails and gear, compasses adjusted, also charts and sailing directions for the voyage, so that you can report in writing that the Steamer is, in your opinion, in every way fit for the service intended. It is advisable that all Ships should have 60 fathoms of 8-inch manilla rope at each end of the Vessel for the exclusive use of tugs, and four 90-fathom lengths of 7-inch manilla warping ropes, i.e., one for each bow and one for each quarter.

2. It must be clearly understood that in the case of stranding, collision, or shifting cargo, your engagement is cancelled, and you will as soon as possible write to the Owners resigning command of the Vessel, to be accepted, or otherwise, according to circumstances.

3. It is equally understood that you receive a bonus of £50 for every 12 months that you are in command without any accident that will cause a claim on the Underwriters of the Ship.

4. Except in special Trades, the agreement with your crew each voyage shall be for a period of three years, for all lawful employment between the parallels of 65 degrees N. and 65 degrees S. Lat., with a victualling scale that can be varied according to climate, etc. and a clause that the seaman and firemen mutually assist in their duties when required. Also, that the crew shall clear out their effects, and thoroughly clean their quarters before leaving the steamer; this to be a condition precedent to payment of wages and discharge. You will be careful to see that the crew's quarters are clean and clear for each fresh crew that joins the steamer.

The following clause to be inserted in all Ships' Articles:—

"In all cases of Salvage Awards, notwithstanding anything herein provided, the rating of the Chief Officer shall be deemed to be the same as that of the Chief Engineer; the rating of the Second Officer that of the Second Engineer; and the Third Officer that of the Third Engineer. Apprentices who have not completed two years' service shall be deemed of the rating of an O.S. and those Apprentices of over two years' service the rating of an A.B."

5. When engaging crews you will in all cases give the preference to British subjects where available, and always pay the wages of the port.

6. The apprentices to be made as comfortable as possible and properly looked after and encouraged to become good and efficient seamen.

7. As the crew's health during the voyage is of the first importance, you should make certain that the forecastles are kept thoroughly clean, and in sickly climates, limewashed and disinfected; also drinking water boiled. Neglect of these precautions has frequently been dearly paid for by prolonged quarantine.

8. You are enjoined to carry out a uniform system of discipline, combining firmness and strictness, with correct bearing and language.

9. In case of accident to your Ship never put into an intermediate port, unless compelled by utter necessity, nor allow yourself to be swayed by your crew to do so, unless convinced of its necessity yourself. It is in such cases of emergency, when energy and perseverance are required that a Captain proves his value to his Owners.

10. When you are obliged to put into a port, never allow yourself to be advised by Agents, who live on the misfortune of Ships, and whose interest it is for you to expend as large a sum as possible. See always whether Messrs.Philipps, Philipps & Co. Ltd., have an Agent in the port before giving away your Ship's business. Never entertain the idea of discharging Cargo, until you are convinced that all other means are useless, such as giving your crew extra wages, shipping extra hands etc. etc.

11. Freight cannot always be claimed on damaged cargo sold at an intermediate port, hence it is always better to put it into the best possible condition, and bring it on. In most cases of survey abroad it will be proper to have the certificate in duplicate, attested by the Consul, one to be sent to Messrs. Philipps, Philipps & Co. Ltd. by post, the other retained on board.

12. Always communicate with the office immediately in case of accident or difficulty, and do not spare a telegram to explain fully your position and meaning.

13. In the event of a serious break down in the Machinery, such as a loss of Screw, breakage of Shaft etc. that cannot be repaired abroad, after making yourself master of the situation, as to what is most advisable to be done, communicate with Messrs. Philipps, Philipps & Co. Ltd. by wire in the fullest possible manner; in such case by your ingenuity and zeal, you will prove your value to all concerned. When telegraphing or writing a description of a breakdown of machinery, it is advisable that the words of the Chief Engineer should be used as nearly as possible in order to avoid technical mistakes which sometimes lead to confusion and delay.

14. In the event of your steamer at any time being in collision, or otherwise doing or receiving any serious damage, please send full particulars of same immediately to our Solicitors, Messrs. Pritchard & Sons, 9 Gracechurch Street, London, E.C., as in case of lawsuit such correspondence is privileged and need not be produced in Court.

15. Should your Vessel be endangered or disabled, and assistance necessary, before accepting assistance make a Stipulated Agreement, if possible. When Boatmen or Steamers see you are firm, they will generally, sooner than lose the chance of helping you, make an Agreement, though at first they may refuse to do so. Should your steamer get stranded and require assistance to refloat, always arrange for same on Lloyds form of Salvage Agreement, if possible. In case your steamer becomes disabled in fine weather show a 3 flag signal to the first passing steamer, and engage for towage to the nearest good port for repairs, if possible for a fixed sum which in your opinion is reasonable in the circumstances. In the case of a breakdown of machinery consult with Chief Engineer before you accept assistance, and ascertain from him if he cannot so repair damage as to enable the vessel to proceed either on her voyage or to the nearest suitable port for repairs.

16. If the weather is bad, and/or your steamer in danger, shew at once the 2 flag urgent signal, and obtain assistance without making any agreement if possible (the reason that in this case you are advised, if possible, not to make any agreement is because the danger being urgent those who offer you assistance may be tempted by your urgent difficulties to take an unfair advantage of the position to obtain a promise of excessive remuneration for their services); but if the weather is such that no immediate assistance can be given, then request the steamer to lay bye, agreeing a sum for such service if required, provided there is reasonable prospect of saving your steamer.

17. Should you fall in with a vessel in fine weather shewing a 3 flag signal for assistance, first examine your Charter and Bill of Lading, to see if "leave to tow" exists, then ascertain the value of disabled vessel and cargo, ascertain also the quantity of coal you have on board and compare it with the distance which the vessel has to be towed: and if towage required, agree for the nearest port on your course, and for such sum as appears reasonable, but not under £500 certain and £5 per mile of towage, for any distance.

18. Should a vessel show a 2 flag signal for towage assistance, at once offer to save life, but on no account attempt salvage, unless your Charter permits, and you can obtain agreement, in proportion to the value of ship and cargo to be salved and risk run.

19. Always offer to take the crew off, and never refuse to lay by, when it appears to you that life may be endangered by leaving the vessel. But, as a general rule, remember that your steamer is not a Tug, and no ordinary towage will cover the risk run.

20. Always look well into your Charter Parties, and Bills of Lading, and see if there be any objectionable clauses; also see that proper clauses are inserted for your Owners' protection, such as negligence clause etc. and have inserted "Ship to have Lien on Cargo for Freight, Dead Freight, Demurrage and Charges"; your Bill of Lading, must recite the Charter on all important points, such as negligence clause etc.; take care that the Bill of Lading signed is that stipulated for in the Charter. In the Black Sea always try and get the 1902 Bill of Lading.

21. On no account accept a letter of indemnity against a clause in Charter or Bill of Lading—such letters are not legal against a third party, and may cause serious loss.

22. Never sign Bills of Lading for Goods until they are Shipped unless you have instructions from your Owners to do so; even when you have seen the goods shipped, refuse to sign until ship receipts (if any) are returned, in exchange for the Bills of Lading; also, never sign for contents, or weight, or condition of any package or Cargo, unless they have been opened, and weighed, or surveyed, in your presence, and qualify them, "Weight and Contents unknown, not answerable for Breakage, Leakage, or Quantity and Quality unknown." Never deliver goods (except under stop) until the Bills of Lading you signed are produced duly endorsed to and by the Receivers.

23. Should the rate of freight be less than the chartered rate, see that the difference is paid before signing the Bill of Lading—otherwise refuse to sign.

24. Insert the correct number of days consumed on the margin of the Bill of Lading, but do not have a smaller number certified than was really spent—rather do without it.

25. Interest and insurance on money advanced, and address commission paid at port of loading, ought to be endorsed on the Bills of Lading. This is a receipt which the receiver of the cargo cannot dispute.

26. You must see that the Vessel's Limbers are clear, Hold thoroughly cleaned and deodorised immediately she is discharged. You must also call upon the Chief Engineer or the Engineer in charge to inspect personally the limbers and pump roses after they have been cleaned under the direction of one of the Deck Officers and before the limber boards are replaced; while at sea, take the greatest care that holds are properly Ventilated, and the steam from the Cargo allowed to escape by opening hatches and using windsails whenever weather permits.

27. As it frequently happens that vessels sail short of their deadweight owing to excessive water left in Bilges and Ballast Tanks, it is of the utmost importance that your officers give their personal attention to the sounding of the Ballast Tanks and Bilges when loading, and report same to you, so that you may if you consider it necessary, verify same yourself.

28. You are expected personally to superintend at sufficient intervals, and give instructions as to the stowage of difficult Cargoes, especially as affecting the trim of the Vessel, taking special care with separations (if any) in grain cargoes, which should, as far as possible, be flat-trimmed. Always prepare a stowage plan, on the forms provided by the office, and forward same prior to sailing. While loading, the Chief Officer to sound round the ship carefully, and make sure the Vessel is always kept afloat.

29. You must be careful that the cargo Books are strictly kept in loading and discharging. A list of all packages in excess, or short landed, must be furnished to your Agent, and a copy sent home to the Owners.

30. No Cargo, Goods, Parcels, Specie, etc. to be carried by any one on board, without paying freight.

31. Always remit freight from abroad by banker's draft, when possible, and, when obtainable, be careful that you have the acceptance of well-known Firms. Remember your Charter says APPROVED BILL on London.

32. A good and approved bill is a bill drawn by one banker and accepted by another banker, and you can demand to have such in settlement of freight. Do not, therefore, take any other bill.

33. Draw money and pay your own bills, or agents will charge large commissions for doing so. On signing accounts for payment see that the utmost discount is allowed, and credit same to the Steamer.

34. Give notice in writing when lay days expire, and claim demurrage, which should be paid day by day. If consignees refuse to do so, and will give no guarantee to pay it on discharge of the cargo, better exercise the lien allowed by Charter, and hold sufficient cargo for security.

35. If the Charter contains no lien for demurrage, then you are not justified in stopping the cargo.

36. Deliver your cargo to no one unless he produces one of the Bills of Lading which you have previously signed; and see that they are properly endorsed by the shipper, or you may be open to an action for wrongful delivery.

37. It will be proper to have a survey of the hatches and dunnage at the port of discharge; and when hatches are opened, to take samples, at a port of call, get a certificate from the merchant's agent that they were in order when opened.

38. When you suspect cargo is damaged give notice to consignees that ship will recognise no claim for such, unless notified before cargo leaves the vessel. If liquids have leaked they should be surveyed before the stowage is broken.

39. When you call at one port for orders to discharge or load at another, ask for your orders in writing, and take care of them; they will be useful in case of dispute.

40. Always keep on good terms with your charterers, shippers, and consignees. Do anything you can to oblige them, consistent with your duty to your Owners. In cases of disputed lay days, demurrage, etc., which cannot be arranged amicably, invite them to arbitration or before the Captain of the Port. Never leave any case of demurrage, etc., unsettled (if possible) before sailing.

41. Protest must be noted immediately on arrival at each port, care being taken to have it extended when necessary.

42. Laid-up returns are recoverable for each consecutive thirty days vessel may lay in port.

43. No account of any description will be acknowledged unless signed by the Captain. No item in Captain's Accounts will be passed without a Voucher.

44. As soon as possible after arrival at a loading or discharging port, telegraph Messrs. Philipps, Philipps & Co. Ltd., when you expect to complete loading or discharging, and should there afterwards be any change in the position of affairs, inform them immediately by telegram.

45. Write to Messrs. Philipps, Philipps & Co. Ltd., each mail, giving full particulars, when likely to complete discharging or loading, actual or estimated freight and expenses, sailing date, etc., and any other information likely to be useful to them.

46. You will be held responsible for the delivery and correctness of all Documents, Papers, Manifests, Official Papers, etc. relative to your ship, Cargo, or Crew, required at each port you may enter; it is therefore incumbent on you, that you make yourself thoroughly acquainted with all that may be required at every port on your route.

47. You will see that your Officers observe with the most scrupulous attention, the Regulations attached to any Harbour or Dock you may go to.

48. Any attempt to evade the Revenue Laws of any Country or Port by any Person in this employ, will lead to the instant dismissal of the offender, and forfeiture of his wages, and it is agreed that he holds himself responsible for any Fines or Losses incurred by the ship.

49. On leaving any port it is your most important duty to make certain that you have sufficient fuel on board to bring the vessel to her next port, with a proper quantity to spare, according to the time of the year, monsoon, or season. It is desirable to get in writing from Engineer note of coals on board and quantity required.

50. You will, with the Chief Engineer, see that the Company's instructions as to the rate of coal consumed per day are carefully adhered to; only in cases of emergency are these instructions to be departed from, and in such cases the reason for doing so to be communicated to the Office.

51. In the Navigation of the Steamer, you are expected to exercise the soundest judgment and caution, the safety of the Vessel being of the first consequence, and next to that, as rapid passages are necessary, you will use the greatest energy, with, however, due regard to the consumption of Fuel.

52. Logs should be hove every two hours, and the Patent Log kept in use. Ship's position ascertained at noon, also during the night when practicable, azimuth and amplitudes every day if possible; Officers to assist you in taking observations, and such observations by Officers to be inspected by you when worked out. Your own working to be kept in ink, so that it can be produced as evidence if required.

53. You are to keep a Night Order Book, and to enter therein all necessary instructions, especially as to course to be steered; should the course have to be altered, it is advisable that you yourself be called to make the alteration, and note it in the Book.

54. Extreme caution to be used to give a sufficiently wide berth, when passing all Headlands, Islands, Shoals, etc, etc. Should the weather be thick or the land obscured, the Engines should be slowed and occasionally stopped, steam whistle sounded, and frequent casts of the lead taken, and the whole minutely recorded in the Log Book. N.B.—You are aware of the importance attached by the Board of Trade to the constant use of the Lead.

55. In foggy weather, use every possible care, as required by the Board of Trade; if in narrow waters, or near land or ice, stop sooner than run any risk.

56. When nearing ice regions, keep a strict look out for bergs and field ice; if night dark and weather thick, test the water by the thermometer every two or three miles; if it lowers suddenly two or three degrees, stop to ascertain the cause. Never enter field ice under any circumstances.

57. You are expected frequently to confer with your Officers as to the Navigation of the Vessel, especially before filling up the night Order Book. It is but prudent that all the Officers should be thoroughly aware of the Ship's position and your ideas and plans. They should have free access to the charts, especially in the vicinity of land.

58. The Deck is never to be left without an Officer in charge on any pretence whatever, and any Officer found off the Deck during his watch or until he is relieved, will be fined half a month's pay. (This to be inserted in the articles).

59. As it is notorious that in too many cases of accident Boats are never ready when required, you are requested to give them personal attention, to have them numbered, every requisite kept on board of them in the most complete order, an Officer and Petty Officer and crew appointed to each and frequently exercised. A special report to be made by the Master from time to time as to the condition of boats and life-saving appliances.

60. No naked light to be taken into Hold or Store Rooms, or about any part of the Ship on any pretence whatever; it is to be inserted in Ship's Articles that any offender consents to a forfeiture of half a month's pay, and for a repeated offence a full month's pay.

61. Entire Ship's Company to have their respective Stations, and to be occasionally exercised in working the pumps, firehoses, buckets, etc. etc., so that in case of outbreak each man may know his station.

62. All orders connected with the Engine Room to pass from yourself to the Chief Engineer, when on duty, or the Engineer on duty; but the Captain will use judgement and not interfere with the working of the engine room, unless in case of disobedience of orders by the Engineer in charge.

63. The vessel should never (where avoidable) be shifted out of her berth while in a harbour or dock without the Master being present. In port the Chief Officer shall have full charge of the Vessel whenever you are on shore. The Ship shall at no time be left without one officer and one Engineer on board in foreign ports. At sea the Officer of the watch shall have full charge when you are below, and they are to be obeyed as having such charge, but they are not to use their authority to interfere with the working either of Engine-room or of the Steward's department. You are to receive the revolutions for the past day at noon from the Chief Engineer, and, in return, will give him the correct distance run by observation or dead reckoning during the same period.

64. Compasses to be adjusted as often as necessary, and in any case, at least once a year.

65. You are expected to make yourself conversant with the new Factory Act rules and to see that their requirements are complied with, especially in connection with cargo gear and the regular testing of same in order to avoid accidents.

66. As primarily responsible for the whole Vessel you are to use wise and proper means to see that the different departments are properly conducted, and to use every endeavour to make all work together for the general good of the Vessel.

67. It is most desirable that all interested should receive the earliest and most frequent information of the Ship's position; you must see that no opportunity is omitted of communicating by signal, or otherwise, with every suitable station or vessel.

68. Abstract of Logs (Deck and Engine), with all remarks of interest as to speed, consumption, conduct of Officers, Engineers, etc., to be sent from each port, for the passage to such port, to the Office by first mail.

69. All receipts for cargo and stores to be signed either in ink or copy-ink pencil.

70. Requisition Lists of all Stores for the ensuing voyage to be prepared (showing surplus stores on board) and forwarded to the Office before sailing from last discharging port.

71. On termination of voyage transmit to the Owners the following papers:—
    (a) Abstract of Ship's Log with any News of the Voyage.
    (b) Requisition Lists of all Repairs, etc. required; duplicate to be sent or handed to the Company's Superintendent.
    (c) List of all Passengers Carried during the Voyage.
    (d) Report upon Condition of Ship and Machinery.
    (e) Report on character and ability of Officers and Engineers.
    (f) Manifests, Copies of Bills of Lading, and Accounts.

DIRECTORS

O. C. Philipps	1889–1931	(Sir O. C. Philipps K.C.M.G. 1909: G.C.M.G. 1918, Baron Kylsant of Carmarthen 1923) (Chairman 1892–1931)
J. W. Philipps	1889–1922	(Baron St. Davids 1908: Viscount St. Davids 1918)
W. D. Sims	1892–1893	
G. Pott	1893–1904	
I. Philipps	1902–1919	(K.C.B. 1918)
W. D. Smallpiece	1906–1920	
D. Davies-Evans	1912–1930	
G. M. Dodd	1918–1940	
Sir F. Vernon Thomson K.B.E.	1921–1953	(Baronet 1938: G.B.E. 1946) (Chairman 1931–1953)
The Hon. G. Coventry	1922–1940	(Viscount Deerhurst 1928: Earl of Coventry 1930)
Baron Suffield	1930–1931	
Percy Cross	1936–1947	
R. B. Thomson	1940–1948 1950–1956	(Chairman 1953–1956)
O. A. Hall	1940–1959	(O.B.E. 1941 Managing Director 1956–1959)
C. Cockroft	1947–1948	
A. M. Campbell	1948–1950	
Sir C. Stuart G.C.M.G; K.B.E.	1948–1956	
C. L. Dalziel	1949–1951	
A. H. Milbourne	1952–1956	
J. S. Bevan	1953–1966	(Chairman 1956–1958)
J. G. Dumsday	1956–1959	
C. C. French	1956–1965	(Managing Director 1960–1965)
R. M. Turnbull	1956–1957	
Hon. A. Cayzer	1957–	
Sir W. N. Cayzer Bt	1958–	(Chairman 1958–)
Viscount Rotherwick	1958–	(Deputy Chairman 1958–)
B. G. S. Cayzer	1962–	
G. B. Jones	1965–1978	(Managing Director 1965–1978)
R. Munton	1970–1972	
A. E. Lemon	1972–1977	
R. A. Morris	1974–	
J. E. Andreae	1978–	
I. B. T. Galloway	1978–	

NOTES: Until 1892 Statutory Meetings of KING LINE LTD. were chaired by James Murray Esq., who was not a Director, while Owen Philipps was described as the Managing Director.

SECRETARIES			ISSUED CAPITAL	
R. A. Braes	1889–1911		1889	£15,680
F. W. Matthews	1911–1952		1893	£20,430
A. G. Preston	1952–1961		1897	£60,000
C. S. Phillips	1961–1973		1899	£150,000
C. H. Lemon	1973–1978		1905	£160,000
K. W. Donald	1978–		1906	£200,000
			1920	£500,000
			1973	£1,000,000

APPENDIX D
Summary of King Line Ltd. Annual Accounts in £'000, 1900–1913; 1915–1959

31st December	Capital and Free Reserve	Fleet Replacement Reserve	Insurance Reserve	Profit and Loss Account Balance	Debentures and Loans	Fleet Value	Investments Value	Net other Assets less other Liabilities	Voyage Profits	Tax (from 1947)
1900	162	—	5	8	—	126	12	37	21	
1901	163	—	5	11	—	122	11	46	25	
1902	157	—	4	6	—	120	16	31	16	
1903	155	—	3	9	—	115	22	30	17	
1904	155	—	2	4	—	114	23	24	6	
1905	164	—	2	6	—	153	29	(10)	11	
1906	202	—	2	9	220	365	29	39	23	
1907	204	—	2	7	213	361	27	38	27	
1908	204	—	2	2	194	358	27	17	17	
1909	204	—	3	2	199	355	26	27	18	
1910	204	—	3	2	192	347	23	31	24	
1911	204	—	2	2	150	334	6	18	42	
1912	220	—	2	6	60	265	5	18	79	
1913	250	—	3	6	50	222	13	74	90	
1915	300	—	5	10	—	* 274		41	102	
1916	400	—	27	20	—	* 209		238	52	
1917	400	—	127	19	—	* 206		340	27	
1918	400	35	128	22	—	* 280		305	55	
1919	450	56	151	25	—	* 711		(29)	70	
1920	750	—	151	26	—	* 987		(60)	95	
1921	750	—	152	30	—	*1028		(96)	96	
1922	750	—	152	30	—	*1009		(77)	40	
1923	750	—	152	40	—	* 938		4	65	
1924	750	—	152	40	—	* 916		26	72	
1925	750	—	152	40	—	* 892		50	51	
1926	750	—	153	40	—	* 898		45	66	
1927	750	—	153	40	800	*1685		58	56	
1928	750	—	137	40	800	*1658		69	69	
1929	750	—	128	40	800	1090	323	305	163	
1930	750	—	126	40	800	1084	324	308	47	
1931	600	—	27	40	711	1012	153	213	41	
1932	600	—	25	25	622	975	231	66	44	
1933	600	—	25	25	533	927	89	167	42	
1934	600	—	25	26	404	927	88	40	25	
1935	600	—	25	23	444	895	79	118	52	
1936	600	—	27	23	444	822	70	202	103	
1937	600	—	27	23	—	603	69	(22)	213	
1938	600	—	29	71	—	522	134	44	198	
1939	625	—	30	79	—	423	133	178	73	
1940	650	144	30	81	—	317	214	374	92	
1941	650	144	32	84	—	273	235	402	84	
1942	650	341	32	84	—	177	235	695	44	
1943	650	354	32	90	—	136	553	437	38	
1944	650	488	32	101	—	80	761	430	59	
1945	650	543	33	139	—	252	1084	29	42	
1946	750	490	35	179	—	426	819	209	225	38
1947	1000	490	37	179	—	394	803	509	483	—
1948	††1500	490	37	201	—	342	682	1204	375	178
1949	1500	490	49	329	—	303	671	1394	250	98
1950	1500	490	69	452	—	441	1872	198	276	83
1951	1900	535	80	457	—	805	1855	312	913	372
1952	2000	535	82	464	—	1001	1838	242	1402	556
1953	2000	850	85	311	—	1054	1841	351	460	132
1954	2000	1100	85	218	—	939	2353	111	495	133
1955	2000	1593	85	209	—	**1714	1767	406	624	264
1956	2000	2298	85	305	—	2143	2914	(369)	1487	691
1957	2000	2079	85	312	—	3188	3309	(2021)	1393	657
1958	2000	2224	85	547	—	3588	664	604	287	103
1959	2000	2330	85	559	—	64	195	4715	(5)	(87)

Notes

1. Capital and Free Reserves
†† The increase in 1948 is attributable to £400,000 profits realised on sale of investments and £100,000 transfer from Profit and Loss Account.

2. Fleet
(a)** The increase in fleet value in 1955 arose from a change in the basis of calculation of depreciation, resulting in a writeback of £764,000.

(b)*The Balance Sheets from 1915–1928 showed a combined amount for fleet and investments. From 1923–1928 this amount further included cash on deposit, otherwise forming part of "Net Other Assets less Other Liabilities".

GENEALOGICAL

1. Simplified Family Tree from 1089.

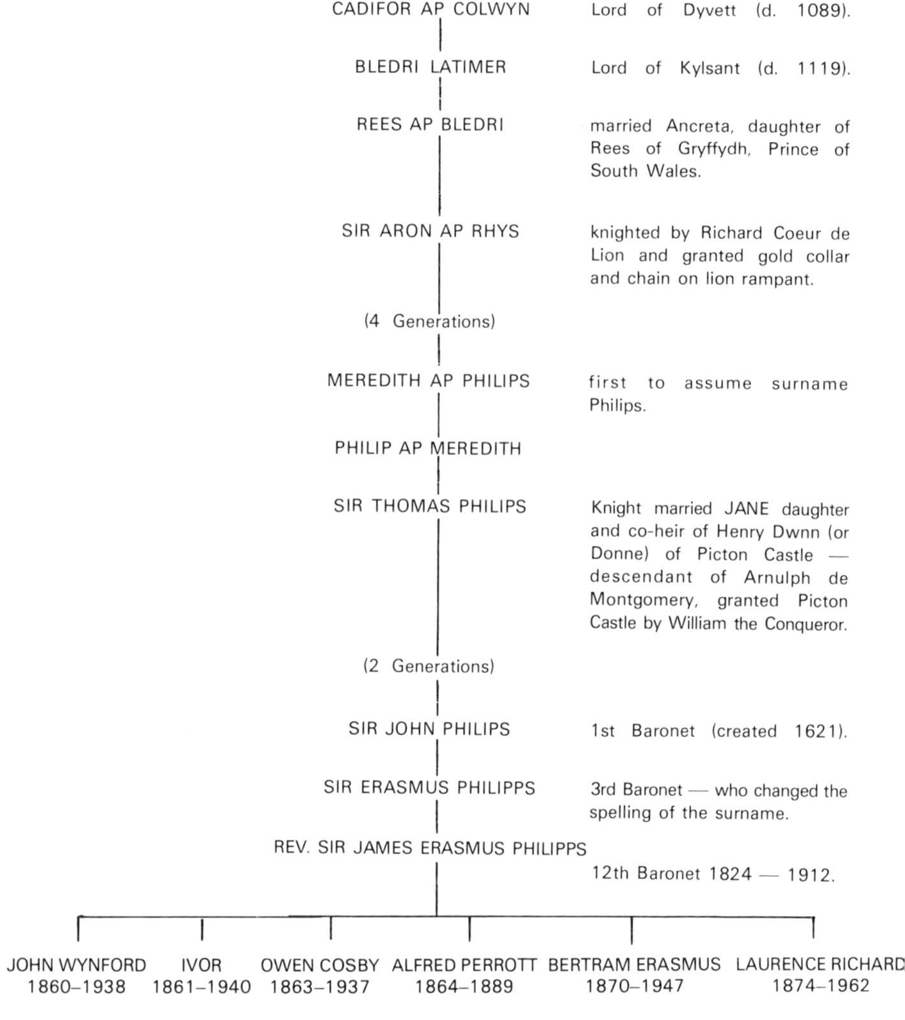

and 5 daughters, the eldest of whom was born in 1866.

Of the above, John Wynford was actively engaged in business with Owen Cosby. Ivor served as Director of King Line for some years and Laurence Richard founded Court Line Ltd.

Lord Kylsant had three daughters of whom the Hon. Mrs. N. D. Fisher-Hoch and the Hon. Mrs. O. C. Barker survive.

2. Names of Ships

Name	First Used	Derivation
ALEXANDER	1952	Three Kings of Scotland between 1107–1286.
ALFRED	1889	9th Century King of Wessex and the only British Monarch to be accorded the title "Great". Name actually adopted for Alfred Perrott Philipps.
ARTHUR	1894	Late 5th Century Romano-British military leader and victor of 12 battles against the invading Anglo-Saxons.
BLEDDYN	1894	Succeeded his half-brother Gruffydd ap Llewellyn 1063 as King of Wales under vassalage of Edward the Confessor. Highly praised for his wisdom and justice in contemporary Welsh chronicles. He was murdered in 1075.
CADWALLON	1894	Exiled by Edwin of Deira 632 but returned and defeated him in alliance with Penda of Mercia. Killed in battle at Hexham by Oswald of Bernicia in 633. Extensively chronicled by Bede.
CHARLES	1957	Two 17th Century Kings of Great Britain.
DAVID	1895	Two Kings of Scotland between 1124–1371. The probability is that this name was actually adopted in honour of St. David Patron Saint of Wales as "Scottish S.S. Co." was not incorporated until 1896.
EDGAR	1896	King of Scotland 1097–1107 — son of Malcolm III and Queen (St.) Margaret. Also Edgar of Wessex crowned at Bath in 973 as first King of all England.
EDWARD	1906	Name of three Pre-Conquest and six Post-Conquest Kings of England up to 1553, subsequently two 20th Century Kings of the United Kingdom. Name probably adopted for reasons topical in 1906.
EDWIN	1927	Early King of Deira and founder of Edinburgh.
EGBERT	1927	Early 9th Century King of Wessex.
FREDERICK	1897	No British King bearing this name is known and it was probably adopted in order to maintain an alphabetical sequence.
GEORGE	1957	Six Kings of United Kingdom 1714–1952.
GRUFFYDD	1898	King of Gwynnedd and Powys and from 1055 King of all Wales. Defeated in battle 1062 by Harold Godwineson, Earl of Wessex (later Harold II) and murdered 1063. Succeeded by Bleddyn ap Cynfyn.
HENRY	1958	Eight Kings of England 1100–1547.
HOWEL	1906	Howel Dda (the Good) died 950. Married daughter of last Prince of Dyfed gaining Pembrokeshire as dowry. Succeeded Idwal Foel as King of Powys. Was succsssful in maintaining peace with the English and was only Welsh Prince to mint his own silver pennies. Went on pilgrimage to Rome in 928 and was responsible for codification of Welsh Law.
IDWAL	1906	King of Powys, died 942.
JAMES	1925	Five Kings of Scotland and two Kings of Great Britain.
JOHN	1906	John Balliol – awarded Scottish Crown by Edward I in 1291 – abdicated 1296 and died 1313. John Plantagenet King of England 1199–1216. Signed Magna Carta. Name probably adopted in honour of John Wynford Philipps.
LUD	1906	Brother of Cassivelaunus and pre-Roman King. Ludgate in the City of London commemorates his name.
MALCOLM	1906	Four Kings of Scotland up to 1165 of whom Malcolm III Ceann Mor (Big Head) (1057–1093) son of Duncan, successor of Macbeth, brother of Donald Bane, husband of St. Margaret and father of Edgar I is best known.
NEPTUNE	1928	Roman God of the Sea.
RICHARD	1975	Three Kings of England 1189–1485. Richard I Coeur de Lion, knighted Sir Aron ap Rhys (Philipps) for valour during the Crusades and granted the right to add a gold collar and chain to the Philipps Lion Rampant.
ROBERT	1926	Three Kings of Scotland 1306–1406. Robert I son of the Bruce was victor at Bannockburn. Robert II was the first King of the House of Stuart.
STEPHEN	1928	King of England 1135–1154.
WILLIAM	1928	William the Lion, King of Scotland 1165–1214. William the Conqueror, King of England 1066–1087, the last successful invader of the British Isles and three subsequent Kings, two being Kings of Great Britain.
BARNSTABLE	1902	Named for Barnstable County, Massachusetts, home of many Boston Fruit Co. executives.
BROOKLINE	1902	Residence of Andrew M. Preston, Manager of the Boston division of the Boston Fruit Co.
MEXICANO	1902	Presumably of geographic significance.

Additionally two further KING names were suggested for vessels completed in 1962–1963 but eventually not so named.

Name		Derivation
CANUTE	not used	Son of Sweyn Forkbeard who succeeded Ethelred the Unready in 1016. He is remembered for the episode when he sat at the sea-shore and vainly instructed the tide to cease flowing, the object not being an exercise in conceit but rather to emphasise to his sycophantic courtiers that he was not as infallible as they seemed to think he wished them to believe.
HAROLD	not used	Son of Godwin, Earl of Wessex and virtual ruler of England during the last years of Edward the Confessor whom he succeeded in January 1066. Defeated Gruffydd of Wales in 1062. In September 1066 he defeated his brother Tostig and Harold Haarfagre at Stamford but was defeated the following month at Hastings by William Duke of Normandy, fighting valiantly to the end.

BARNSTABLE	10	KING ARTHUR 1	3	KING GRUFFYDD 1	8		
BROOKLINE	11	2	13	2	27		
DON ARTURO	E1	3	23	KING HENRY	55		
DON BENITO	E2	4	42	KING HOWEL 1	19		
DON CESAR	E3	5	52	2	30		
DON DIEGO	E4	KING BLEDDYN 1	2	KING IDWAL 1	18		
DON EMILIO	E5	2	14	2	31		
EMPIRE ANTIGUA	D17	3	25	KING JAMES 1	33		
EMPIRE BENEFIT	D9	KING CADWALLON 1	4	2	49		
EMPIRE BOMBARDIER	D7	2	12	3	57		
EMPIRE COMET	D1	3	28	KING JOHN 1	20		
EMPIRE EARL	D14	KING CHARLES 1	53	2	39		
EMPIRE HOUSMAN	D12	2	59	KING LUD 1	21		
EMPIRE LATIMER	D2	KING DAVID 1	5	2	40		
EMPIRE MIST	D5	2	16	KING MALCOLM 1	22		
EMPIRE RAY	D13	3	26	2	34		
EMPIRE TAVOY	D16	4	46	3	50		
FORST	C3	KING EDGAR 1	6	KING NEPTUNE	41		
FORT AKLAVIK	D8	2	36	KING RICHARD	60		
FORT CARILLON	D10	3	47	KING ROBERT 1	35		
FORT FRANKLIN	D4	KING EDWARD 1	15	2	48		
FORT NASHWAAK	D6	2	32	KING STEPHEN	43		
FORT ST. REGIS	D11	KING EDWIN	37	KING WILLIAM 1	44		
GERA	C4	KING EGBERT	38	2	58		
ISIS	C1	KING FREDERICK 1	7	MEXICANO	9		
KING ALEXANDER	51	2	17	OCEAN CRUSADER	D3		
KING ALFRED 1	1	3	29	SAMGLORY	D15		
2	24	KING GEORGE 1	54	TANNENBERG	C2		
3	45	2	61				
4	56						

APPENDIX F

ACKNOWLEDGEMENTS

This book has only been possible thanks to the information supplied by a great many people, to all of whom I am most grateful.

The basis of the narrative has been the Minute Books and Annual Accounts of King Line Ltd., and I record my thanks to the Directors for allowing me full access; also for permission to reprint the Instructions to Masters. I am also obliged to Sir W. Nicholas Cayzer, Bt., for kindly writing a foreword.

Further information has come from former members of the sea and shore staff, and these contributions are, in the main, acknowledged in the text. However, in addition to these specific items, other items of a more general nature were provided, and in this respect I wish to refer, in addition to those named in the text, to help received from former Engineer Superintendent Lindsay Dryden, for technical details, and to Messrs. R. A. Morris, G. B. Jones, and C. Lemon for their help.

I wish particularly to thank Captains G. F. Smith O.B.E., and J. A. Lewis, also the late J. S. Bevan, who from the outset took a deep interest in the progress of this history, and provided many valuable memories coupled with a meticulous eye for detail and accuracy. Sadly, he died shortly after the penultimate draft had been circulated for comment.

I have also received assistance from members of the Philipps family, in particular Lord Kylsant's daughters The Hon. Mrs. N. D. Fisher-Hoch J.P., D.L., and The Hon. Mrs. O. C., Barker J.P., also from Messrs. G. Thum, M. Middlebrook, the editors of Fairplay and Sea Breezes, and Dr. P. N. Davies, who is the author of a biography of Lord Kylsant, to be published by Europa Business Publications in the near future.

I record my thanks to Mr. P. Markham for permission to reproduce his copyright account of his incarceration in the Argentine Republic while serving as a Cadet.

Technical research has been with the help of the staff of Lloyds Register, the National Maritime Museum, and the Central Record of the World Ship Society, especially Messrs. M. Crowdy, J. Lingwood, and H. Appleyard.

I have been fortunate in having a wide choice of photographs. It has not been possible to use them all, those which are published are credited in situ. I am grateful to all who helped with photographs and plans.

Finally, I record my thanks to Lord Tennyson for providing a title, and to the ladies who typed the many drafts. Credit for this work rightly belongs to my contributors and helpers, I can only claim to be responsible for any errors and omissions.